RISK
happens!

To John
Best Regards
Mike.

MIKE CLAYTON

RISK
happens!

MANAGING RISK AND AVOIDING FAILURE IN BUSINESS PROJECTS

Copyright © 2011 Mike Clayton

Published by Marshall Cavendish Business
An imprint of Marshall Cavendish International

PO Box 65829
London EC1P 1NY
United Kingdom
info@marshallcavendish.co.uk

and

1 New Industrial Road
Singapore 536196
genrefsales@sg.marshallcavendish.com
www.marshallcavendish.com/genref

Marshall Cavendish is a trademark of Times Publishing Limited

Other Marshall Cavendish offices:
Marshall Cavendish International (Asia) Private Limited, 1 New Industrial Road, Singapore 536196 . Marshall Cavendish Corporation, 99 White Plains Road, Tarrytown NY 10591-9001, USA . Marshall Cavendish International (Thailand) Co Ltd, 253 Asoke, 12th Floor, Sukhumvit 21 Road, Klongtoey Nua, Wattana, Bangkok 10110, Thailand . Marshall Cavendish (Malaysia) Sdn Bhd, Times Subang, Lot 46, Subang Hi-Tech Industrial Park, Batu Tiga, 40000 Shah Alam, Selangor Darul Ehsan, Malaysia

The right of Mike Clayton to be identified as the author of this work has been asserted by him in accordance with the Copyright, Designs and Patents Act 1988.

All rights reserved

No part of this publication may be reproduced, stored in a retrieval system or transmitted, in any form or by any means, electronic, mechanical, photocopying, recording or otherwise, without the prior permission of the copyright owner. Requests for permission should be addressed to the publisher.

The authors and publisher have used their best efforts in preparing this book and disclaim liability arising directly and indirectly from the use and application of this book. All reasonable efforts have been made to obtain necessary copyright permissions. Any omissions or errors are unintentional and will, if brought to the attention of the publisher, be corrected in future printings.

A CIP record for this book is available from the British Library

ISBN 978-981-4328-30-2

Cover design by OpalWorks

Printed and bound in the United Kingdom by TJ International

For my father, Gerald Clayton,
whose attitude to risk still affects my every decision

CONTENTS

List of Tables and Figures		ix
Acknowledgements		xiii
Prologue		xv
Chapter 1	Introduction	1
Chapter 2	Planning Out Risk	9
Chapter 3	The Risk Management Process	30
Chapter 4	Identify Risks	40
Chapter 5	Analyse Risks	59
Chapter 6	Plan for Risks	85
Chapter 7	Take Action on Risks	97
Chapter 8	Risk Monitoring and Control	104
Chapter 9	Risk Resilience	119
Chapter 10	Involving Stakeholders in Risk Management	124
Chapter 11	Appetite for Risk	133
Chapter 12	The Psychology of Risk	142
Chapter 13	Risk Culture	151
Conclusion		160
Appendix A	List of Common Project Risks	161
Appendix B	Glossary	165
Appendix C	Learn More	173

TABLES AND FIGURES

Tables

Table 1.1	Why Crises Happen	3
Table 2.1	Estimating Techniques	21
Table 2.2	Common Estimating Errors and Omissions	22
Table 3.1	Variables of Scale and Complexity for Your Risk Management Process	33
Table 3.2	Drivers of Scale and Complexity for Your Risk Management Process	33
Table 3.3	Sample Roles and Responsibilities for Project Risk Management	34
Table 3.4	Reasons for Documenting Aspects of Your Risk Management Process	38
Table 3.5	Typical Contents of a Risk Management Plan	38
Table 4.1	Core Project Documents	43
Table 4.2	Typical Considerations for a Project Risk Potential Review	44
Table 4.3	Indicative Risk Kick-off Workshop Agenda	46
Table 4.4	Risk Identification Using Personal Experience	48
Table 4.5	SPECTRES	49
Table 4.6	Risk Categories	51
Table 4.7	Risk Register – Part 1	56
Table 4.8	Formal Description of a Risk	57

Table 5.1	Typical Descriptors for Likelihood	64
Table 5.2	Typical Probability Ranges for Likelihood	65
Table 5.3	Suggested Probability Ranges for Likelihood	66
Table 5.4	Suggested General Scales for Impact	66
Table 5.5	Suggested Scales for Schedule Impact	67
Table 5.6	Suggested Scales for Financial Impact	67
Table 5.7	Suggested Scales for Quality Impact	67
Table 5.8	Suggested Scales for Scope Impact	68
Table 5.9	Suggested Scales for Reputational Impact	68
Table 5.10	Suggested Scales for Health, Safety or Security Impact	68
Table 5.11	Suggested Scales for Environmental Impact	68
Table 5.12	Frequently Used Numerical Scale for Likelihoods and Impacts	69
Table 5.13	Example of an Exponential Numerical Scale for Likelihoods and Impacts	71
Table 5.14	Failings of Risk Scoring Systems	71
Table 5.15	Traffic Light Status Definitions	73
Table 5.16	(a) RMS Method – Risk 1	77
	(b) RMS Method – Risk 2	78
	(c) RMS Method – Calculation	78
	(d) RMS Method – Results	78
Table 5.17	Risk Register – Part 2	83
Table 6.1	Tactics to Remove Project Risk	87
Table 6.2	Tactics to Reduce the Likelihood of Project Risk	88
Table 6.3	Tactics to Reduce the Impact of Project Risk	89
Table 6.4	Contingency Planning Process	90
Table 6.5	Elements of a Contingency Plan for Project Risk	91
Table 6.6	Risk Response Plan	94
Table 6.7	Risk Register – Part 3	95
Table 7.1	Risk Register – Part 4	102
Table 8.1	Leading Indicators of Project Risk	106

Table 8.2	Crashing the Timeline	111
Table 9.1	Scenario Planning Process	121
Table 9.2	Business Continuity Management Process	123
Table 10.1	The Stages of Resistance to Change	125
Table 10.2	Examples of Project Stakeholders	129
Table 10.3	Factors Affecting Stakeholders' Attitudes to Risk	130
Table 10.4	Project Communication Strategy	131
Table 10.5	Stakeholder Communication Plan	131
Table 11.1	Typical Factors leading to a High Risk Project	136
Table 13.1	Typical Benefits of a Strong Risk Management Culture	151
Table 13.2	Elements of a Strong Organisational Risk Culture	153
Table 13.3	Steps in Creating a Strong Organisational Risk Culture	154
Table 13.4	Risk Management Maturity Levels	155
Table 13.5	Lessons Learned Register	157
Table 13.6	Post-Project Risk Review	158

Figures

Figure 1.1	Risk Mirror	2
Figure 1.2	Project Risk Management	6
Figure 2.1	Project Cost-Risk Profile	9
Figure 2.2	Time-Cost-Quality Triangle	11
Figure 2.3	Time-Cost-Quality-Scope	12
Figure 2.4	Scope	13
Figure 2.5	Risk Breakdown Structure	14
Figure 2.6	Scope Creep and Defining Scope	15
Figure 2.7	Work Breakdown Structure	16
Figure 2.8	Product Breakdown Structure	17
Figure 2.9	RACI Chart	18

Figure 2.10	PERT Estimates	23
Figure 2.11	Slippage in Highly Dependent Tasks	24
Figure 2.12	Islands of Stability in a Project Schedule	25
Figure 2.13	Cost and Organisational Breakdown Structure	26
Figure 3.1	The Risk Management Process	30
Figure 3.2	Core Risk Management Documents	37
Figure 4.1	Periodic Review to Identify New Risks	41
Figure 4.2	Starting Place for Identifying Project Risks	42
Figure 4.3	SWOT Analysis	49
Figure 4.4	Fishbone Diagram	52
Figure 4.5	Fishbone Diagram – Stage 2	52
Figure 4.6	Process Decision Programme Chart	54
Figure 4.7	The Formal Structure of a Risk	57
Figure 5.1	Likelihood versus Impact Chart	69
Figure 5.2	Likelihood versus Impact Chart, with Scoring	70
Figure 5.3	Risk Dependency Map	72
Figure 5.4	Likelihood versus Impact Chart, with Colour Zones	72
Figure 5.5	Time to Impact versus Likelihood, with Bubble Size Representing Impact	75
Figure 5.6	Time to Impact versus Complexity, with Bubble Size Representing Impact	75
Figure 5.7	Likelihoods of 2 Independent Events, with Bubble Size Representing Impact of Combined Outcome	76
Figure 5.8	Budget Impact versus Schedule Impact, with Bubble Size Representing Probability	76
Figure 5.9	Decision Tree Example	79
Figure 5.10	The Beta Function	80
Figure 5.11	Examples of Statistical Distributions	81
Figure 5.12	The "Sleep at Night Test" Results	83
Figure 6.1	When to Do Risk Planning	86
Figure 6.2	Contingency Planning Process	90
Figure 6.3	More Research in Your Risk Management Process	93

Figure 7.1	Take Action on Risks	98
Figure 7.2	Consequential Risks Arise from Treating an Existing Risk	101
Figure 8.1	Risk Monitoring and Control	104
Figure 8.2	Earned Value Analysis	105
Figure 8.3	Risk Reporting – Scatter Plot	107
Figure 8.4	Risk Reporting – Trend Analysis	108
Figure 8.5	Risk Reporting – Category Analysis	109
Figure 8.6	Time–Cost–Quality–Scope	110
Figure 9.1	Scenario Analysis	120
Figure 9.2	Scenario Planning	120
Figure 9.3	Business Continuity Management	122
Figure 10.1	Predicted Efficiency Gains Following Project Handover	126
Figure 10.2	Observed Efficiency Gains and Losses Around Project Handover	126
Figure 10.3	Stakeholder Management Process	128
Figure 11.1	Risk Appetite	134
Figure 11.2	Personality Driven by Attitudes to Uncertainty and Consequences	137
Figure 11.3	Risk Managers in Context	138
Figure 11.4	Threat and Benefit Analysis for Potential Projects	140

ACKNOWLEDGEMENTS

I COULD NOT HAVE written this book without the opportunities afforded me to manage projects and learn about risk by colleagues at Deloitte Consulting, where I worked from the early 1990s until 2002. In particular, I am grateful to Gilbert Toppin, Brian Green, John Everett, George Owen, Tricia Bey, Chris Loughran and Richard Porter. I also gained valuable insights about risk from many other colleagues – particularly Mark Warren, Charles Vivian and John Perry (whose article I rediscovered in preparing this book).

There are also a number of project management bloggers whom I must thank for their insights. Often, their thinking is at a level well above that of this book, so my apologies to them, if a whole blog, or even series of blogs, has informed just one sentence, or simply the way I express an idea. The details are important to me, so thank you in particular to Glen Alleman, Kailash Awati and John Goodpasture.

I must also thank my wife, Felicity, who gave me the time to write this and read the manuscript carefully, with the eye of a risk management novice – the readership for whom the book is intended. She made me work just a little harder to explain what sometimes seemed obvious to someone inside the industry.

PROLOGUE

EVE IS A 52-YEAR-OLD WOMAN living in Britain today. She attends a routine breast cancer screening at her local hospital and is shocked to get a letter calling her back for further tests – her screening results are positive. Eve urgently looks for information and finds plenty of facts on the Cancer Research UK website. Around 260 out of every 100,000 women in the 50–55 year age bracket have breast cancer. Screening will detect their cancer in around 85% of cases. In about 10% of all cases, a positive result is a false reading and there is no cancer.

How worried should Eve be? In Eve's place, most of us would be very worried indeed. Many would rate Eve's chance of having cancer at 70%, 80% or even 90%. This is a case of our intuitions about statistical risk letting us down badly. Let us analyse the situation step-by-step, to understand the real level of risk to Eve.

If 100,000 women in Eve's age range are screened, we expect that 260 of them will actually have breast cancer. The statistics tell us that 85% of those cancers will be detected – that is, 221 women. Of the remaining 99,740 women who don't have the cancer, 10% will receive a false positive result on their first screening – this means 9,974 worried women with no cancer.

We are now ready to look at the important statistics. Of the 100,000 women who were tested, 10,195 of them were called back for further tests. That is, 221 women who really have breast cancer and 9,974 who don't. This means 221 out of 10,195, or just over 2% of the women called back will have cancer. So Eve has a 1:46 chance of having breast cancer. This is worrying, but far from a certainty, and more important for us, a long way from the level of likelihood that many people would have estimated.

RISK RARELY MATCHES OUR INTUITIONS

Shift happens. Things go wrong in our lives, but neither our mental wiring, nor our basic education, nor even the majority of our life experiences prepare us well to understand and handle risk. If Eve's case shows us anything, it is that we need to work hard to understand the level of risk we face; and this is doubly so when we have choices about how to respond.

Increasingly, many of us are involved in making change happen – in our workplace, in our communities and in our homes. Projects are becoming a way of life, and the faster we make change happen, the more uncertainty we have to deal with. At the core of project management is the management of risk. *Risk Happens!* is not a book about project management, but you will learn a lot about project management from it. *Risk Happens!* is a book about managing project risk. For anyone needing to undertake a new venture, this is essential.

CHAPTER 1
INTRODUCTION

IF YOU ARE MANAGING A PROJECT, then risk management is an essential part of your tool set, and more and more of us are becoming project managers. This book is aimed at project managers in private business, the public sector, the voluntary sector, local communities and in the home. I have written it to be of value to the widest audience, from novices and students to experienced project managers.

This book is not aimed at experienced managers of large scale capital projects or where severe risks warrant advanced mathematical techniques and the highest standards of formality. If you have been managing projects for many years and want to understand these advanced techniques, you will need to look elsewhere, to more technical books. But before you do, please take a look at *Risk Happens!* There is a lot in this book that may jog your memory, stimulate new ideas and refresh your thinking.

For everyone who reads this book, you will gain a simple, powerful process for managing risk, a big basket of tools to help you and some thought-provoking insights into the context of project risk and how we respond to it.

WHAT IS PROJECT RISK?

A risk is something that may or may not happen. If it does happen, it will have an effect on your project. So, the nature of risk is outlined in two concepts:

2 RISK HAPPENS!

- it is an uncertain event
- it causes a change in your project.

Project risk is therefore uncertain events that can affect outcomes.

Notice that, in this definition, risk can introduce positive or negative changes. Whilst we often think of risks as having adverse consequences, it can also present positive opportunities. Threat and opportunity are like mirror images. This book will, of course, address the opportunities that harness benefits, but it will focus mainly on the threat posed by risk.

Figure 1.1: Risk Mirror

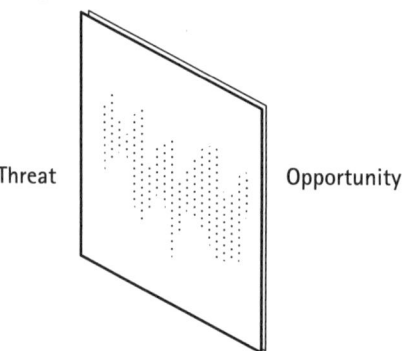

Threat   Opportunity

A Hierarchy of Risks

When you consider the definition of risk and the task that project risk management faces, there is a bewildering array of concepts. Don't worry. They are easily distinguished, and even more reassuringly, the distinctions rarely matter in the day-to-day practical task of managing your project and getting things done. So let us look at three ways the term "project risk" can be used and examine what we mean by each.

- *A project risk* – This is an individual risk that can affect one part of your project.
- *Project risks* – These are individual risks that can affect the whole of your project.
- *Project risk* – This is the overall level of uncertainty of outcome for your whole project.

WHY IS RISK IMPORTANT TO PROJECT MANAGERS?

Project managers set out to deliver their products, services or change within pre-established deadlines while facing the uncertainties inherent in a new project. Two things will help you in this endeavour: plans and controls. When a project is under-planned and poorly controlled, it will surely fail.

Plans and Controls

Plans set out how you intend to deliver your project. They address the three project elements: tasks, time and resources; and describe what needs to be done, how it will be done, when, by whom, with what assets and materials and how it will be paid for. Sadly, the uncaring universe will not respect your plan. US President Eisenhower is credited with the dictum: "Plans are worthless, but planning is everything." The truth of this statement is well-known to all project managers.

Controls establish two things: how you propose to stick to your plan in the face of the challenges of the real world, and what you will do when reality forces your project to deviate from plan. Risk management is, perhaps, the most important of your project controls.

Crises happen when we cannot respond effectively to a threat. They are rarely due to a lack of plans or processes. Rather, they tend to be the result of overconfidence and complacency. Table 1.1 sets out some examples.

Table 1.1: Why Crises Happen

Crises most often happen due to overconfidence, which can lead to an inability to detect key threats. Project managers can be overconfident:
- in predicting outcomes
- in planning
- in systems and processes
- in people

more >>>

- in assessing random or unpredictable events, like the weather
- in missing small but significant changes
- in failing to notice outside influences
- in failing to predict the possibility of human error/human weaknesses
- in being deaf to warnings

More Reasons Why Projects Fail: Strategic Risk Factors

Over the years, many organisations have researched the risk factors that indicate potential project failure. They do this by surveying failed projects and asking those involved or external observers for their assessment of the reasons for failure. The reasons that emerge have a depressingly familiar ring to anyone who has spent much time working in an organisational context. Here are the top 10 risk factors, in no particular order. This book will address all of these risks.

1. The project goal and objectives are either unclear, or are disconnected from the organisation's other priorities, leading to a weak case for change.
2. People have unrealistic expectations, leading to a determination of failure despite the project meeting its goal and objectives.
3. Senior people in leadership roles fail to accept responsibility for the project, and do not give it the support, commitment and leadership it needs. This often leads to an over-reliance on consultants or outside contractors.
4. People resist the changes that the project brings or resist participating in the process, often because their role in the project's success is undervalued by the team.
5. Project management, change management, stakeholder management and risk management skills are lacking.
6. The project is poorly planned, without a sound basis for estimates of schedule and resources, leading to unrealistic deadlines or budget.
7. Key elements of the project are not controlled effectively, such as

changes to scope or functionality, delivery or quality of products, or deviations from plan.
8. There is too much focus on cost – or price of contracts – and not enough on the balance between cost and risk/value.
9. A project solution is defined before adequate research has validated that it is technically possible, organisationally desirable and free of unintended consequences.
10. Project overload – the organisation is simply trying to do too much with the resources that it has available.

WHAT IS PROJECT RISK MANAGEMENT?

Since all new projects involve, by definition, novelty, innovation and change, there will also be many uncertainties. So project managers have developed ways to maximise control where possible, and minimise the areas where we have no control. Project risk management consists of three things:

1. Processes, systems and procedures that try and make the project more predictable, and bring rigor and accountability to the way we manage uncertainty and its consequences.
2. Tools, techniques and methods that help us understand and deal with the real world, day-to-day.
3. Attitudes, values and perspectives that allow us as humans to cope and to overcome our instinctive responses to uncertainty and crisis.

Management is the Discharge of Responsibility

It is important that we accept that no form of risk management can eliminate all risks. But it is also true, as Peter Bernstein says in his book about the history of financial risk, *Against the Gods*: "If everything is a matter of luck, risk management is a meaningless exercise." If we believe too much in the power of luck, it relieves us of responsibility. With good risk management you cannot prevent shift from happening, but you can reduce the frequency and scale of adverse events.

Figure 1.2: Project Risk Management

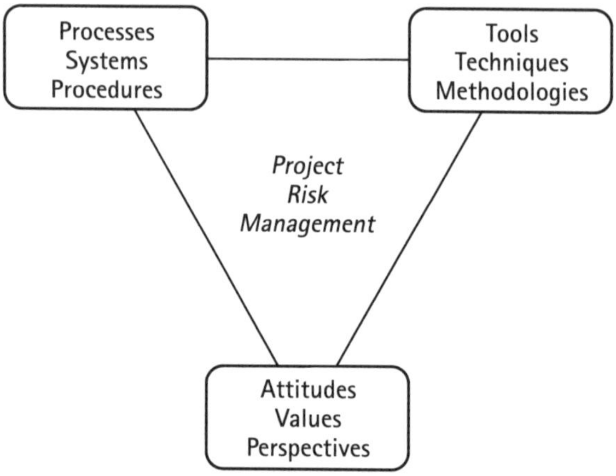

AN OVERVIEW OF *RISK HAPPENS!*

Risk Happens! will provide you with a comprehensive overview of all of the aspects of project risk management.

Chapter 2: Planning Out Risk

Risk management begins with building a robust plan that reduces your risk from the start. Chapter 2 looks at how to define a project with clarity and precision from the outset, and explores the principal project planning tools that allow you to address the key areas of risk: scope, schedule, resources and quality.

Chapter 3: The Risk Management Process

Chapter 3 is the keystone that holds the arch of this book in place. It sets out a fundamental four-stage process for managing project risk and sets that process in an organisational context. You will learn how this process can be scaled for any size of project and level of risk, and discover what are the roles and responsibilities that go with risk management.

Chapter 4: Identify Risks

This chapter will give you a host of techniques to identify project risks by examining the key risk impact areas of quality, scope, schedule and resources, as well as the sources of risk. It includes tips on conducting a project risk workshop and assessing your overall project risk. This chapter will also introduce you to your primary risk management tool, the risk register, and how to describe a risk formally.

Chapter 5: Analyse Risks

Learn how to understand, evaluate, categorise and prioritise the risks you have identified. What risks can you safely ignore and what risks should you focus on? You will learn about how to assess risks qualitatively and quantitatively, and ways to illustrate risks to your colleagues and stakeholders.

Chapter 6: Plan for Risks

There are six principal strategies for managing risk, which you can combine into thousands of detailed approaches. This chapter looks at these six strategies and gives examples of how to apply them.

Chapter 7: Take Action on Risk

The commonest mistake risk managers make is to pay insufficient attention to actively managing risk. This chapter shows you how to focus on practical steps to reduce risk day-to-day. Success requires persistence, so closing the loop in reviewing the outcomes of your actions is vital.

Chapter 8: Risk Monitoring and Control

Complete control requires an active approach to observing what is going on and updating your understanding frequently. In this chapter you will learn about the monitor and control cycle and different ways to respond to problems or opportunities that arise. Another important part of the cycle is ongoing project assurance. Finally, you need to keep others fully informed, so this chapter will also discuss reporting.

Chapter 9: Risk Resilience
Don't just try to avoid risk, build resilience so that you can handle it – even when a perfect storm of risks manifests. This chapter will introduce the disciplines of scenario planning, contingency planning and disaster recovery.

Chapter 10: Involving Stakeholders in Risk Management
Your stakeholders will determine the success – or otherwise – of your project. This chapter shows you the basic tools for involving your stakeholders in a dialogue about project risk.

Chapter 11: Appetite for Risk
How you manage risk will depend on how much risk you are prepared to accept. This chapter explores the strategic aspects of risk management and gives you the tools to prioritise which projects you undertake by reviewing their potential risk and return.

Chapter 12: The Psychology of Risk
Your perception of risk is never objective. A host of psychological factors determine the way we perceive and respond to risks; this chapter explores both individual and group biases.

Chapter 13: Risk Culture
The last chapter looks at the decision making, oversight and policy infrastructure that needs to surround your project. Learn how to incorporate organisational learning into your plan, how to identify lessons from your project, and the basic foundations for building a risk-aware and risk-responsible culture.

CHAPTER 2
PLANNING OUT RISK

PROJECT RISK MANAGEMENT must begin with taking steps to avoid the risks that you can avoid. A clear definition of what your project is – and is not – will avoid unnecessary confusion, and it will form a firm foundation for planning your project.

The second fundamental is to plan your project to remove or reduce the risks you can. At this stage, you will start to face some real choices in how to specify and conduct your project; trading cost for certainty. Figure 2.1 shows how different project solutions typically offer different levels of risk. Your planning process must explicitly choose from among those options.

Figure 2.1: Project cost-risk profile

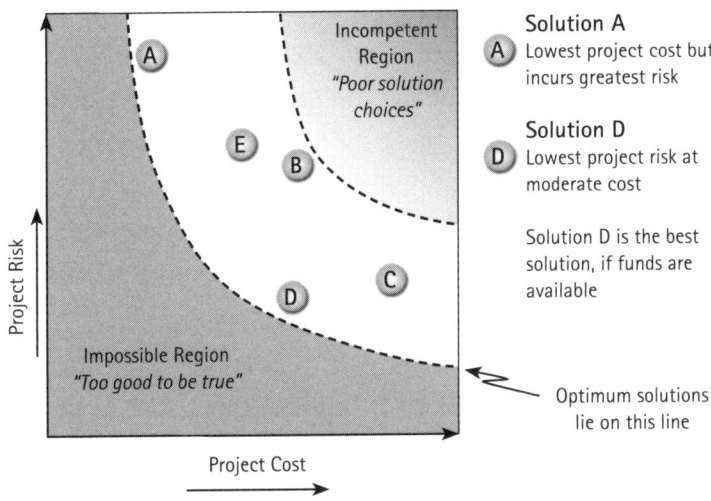

This chapter will give you an introduction to aspects of the definition and planning phases of a project and will offer you a range of ways that you can address scope, schedule, budget and quality risks by the way you plan your project.

PROJECT DEFINITION

Project risk can be defined as uncertainty that can affect outcomes, so your first step in reducing risk is to remove uncertainty. In the earliest stages of your project, start by working hard to remove uncertainty about your project's goal and objectives by consulting widely, then defining and documenting them as clearly and unambiguously as you can.

Step 1: Project Goal

Your project goal states what the project is designed to achieve. The reason for commissioning – or at least considering – your project should therefore be self-evident from your goal. Whilst broad consensus among the project commissioners and clarity of language are the most important things, it is also helpful to craft the wording of your goal so that it creates an enticing prospect for the people you will want to engage as team members, collaborators and supporters.

Step 2: Project Objectives

Once you have a goal agreed, your next negotiation will be to set the project's objectives. These define the measures of success that you will apply to achieve your goal. These are typically measures of:

- **Time**
  Completion targets that can be anything from loose ambitions ("to be completed over the next three years") to tight deadlines ("to be fully operational by 1 July 2015").
- **Cost**
  Cost covers financial and other resource costs, such as people, assets and material. These can all be traded for money.

Planning Out Risk 11

- **Quality**
  Quality will come to the fore when safety is an issue on your project, and also where the reputation of the project's promoter is linked to the success of the project.

Time, cost and quality form the project management Time-Cost-Quality Triangle.

Figure 2.2: Time-Cost-Quality Triangle

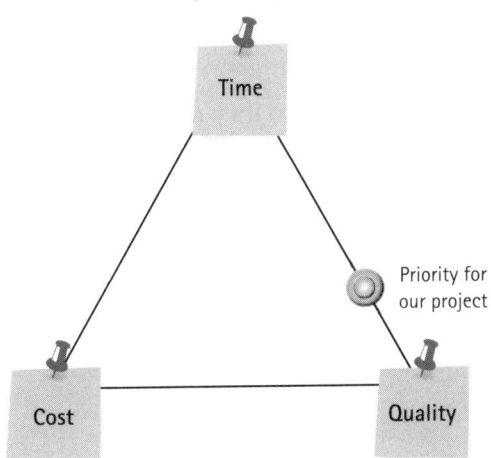

The Time-Cost-Quality Triangle is a powerful tool for a project manager. Right from the outset, having determined your sponsor's objectives, find out where on this triangle their priority lies. It might, as in Figure 2.2, lie between the time and quality values, suggesting that quality is their first concern. You must work hard to deliver this, and once you have delivered this, you must focus on delivering to schedule. Only then, do you seek to optimise the cost.

Notice how these three corners constrain one another. Once your sponsor has set objectives for time and quality and you have calculated an optimum budget, the three corners of your triangle come into balance.

If your sponsor wants the project delivered earlier than planned, you can only do so by committing more money or resources, or by cutting corners on the quality. If they want a higher specification, it will take you longer and cost more. And if they want to drive down cost, you can only do so by compromising quality or taking longer. Alternative names for this triangle are the *Triangle of Balance* or the *Triple Constraint.*

Your ability to trade off one constraint against the others effectively is wholly dependent upon everyone concerned having a shared understanding of the definition of your project.

Step 3: Project Scope

Shift happens and things will go wrong on your project. The wise project manager will build contingencies into their allowances for time-schedule, cost-budget and quality-specification, to allow for problems. But there may also come a time when you run out of contingency... Happily, there is a fourth corner to the Time-Cost-Quality Triangle!

Figure 2.3: Time-Cost-Quality-Scope

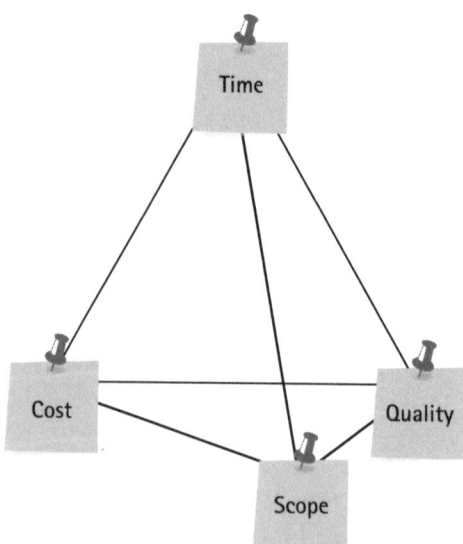

Scope is not about the quality of the assets, products, services or processes your project produces; it is about the quantity. Scope measures how much you plan to deliver. If you run out of time and budget, and cannot cut corners, what remains is your ability to deliver less than originally planned. Scope is a key concept for project managers. If you start your project knowing which elements of scope are of least value to your sponsor, then, when trouble arises, you may be able to scale back aspects of the project without damaging your core goal.

Scope is most easily represented by a boundary. Everything inside this boundary is "in scope" – this is the project's task and the project manager's responsibility. Everything outside the boundary is "out of scope".

Figure 2.4: Scope

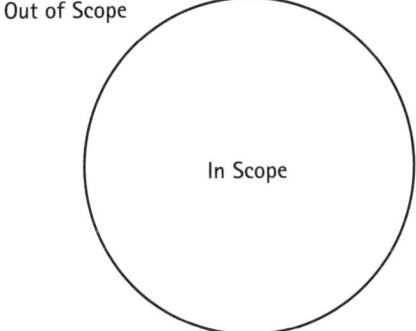

After you have defined you project goal and objectives, the third essential step is defining and agreeing among key people what the scope of your project is and is not.

A Breakdown of the Risks

One of the most powerful tools for identifying risks is to break down all of your project risks according to a fixed set of risk categories. Time, cost, quality and scope offer us one of the most useful ways to identify project risks and we will use these categories to help us to plan out some of the major project risks you are likely to encounter. Presenting risks as a hierarchy in this manner gives us what is known as a Risk Breakdown Structure – sometimes abbreviated to RBS.

Figure 2.5: Risk Breakdown Structure

```
                              Project
        ┌──────────────┬─────────────┬──────────────┐
      1 Time         2 Cost       3 Quality       4 Scope
        │              │              │              │
  1.1 Technical    2.1 Procurement  3.1 Component  4.1 Scope creep
      delays                           failure
        │              │              │              │
  1.2 Key person   2.2 Interest     3.2 Surface    4.2 Definition
      loss             rate             finish
        │              │              │              │
  1.3 Decision     2.3 Exchange     3.3 Life       4.3 Second language
      delays           rate             expectancy
        │              │              │              │
  1.4 Dependencies 2.4 Commodity    3.4 Materials  4.4 Parts unavailable
                       prices           defects
        │              │              │              │
  1.5 Recruitment  2.5 Skills loss  3.5 Software   4.5 Regulatory change
                                        defects
        │              │              │              │
      1.6 ...        2.6 ...         3.6 ...        4.6 ...
```

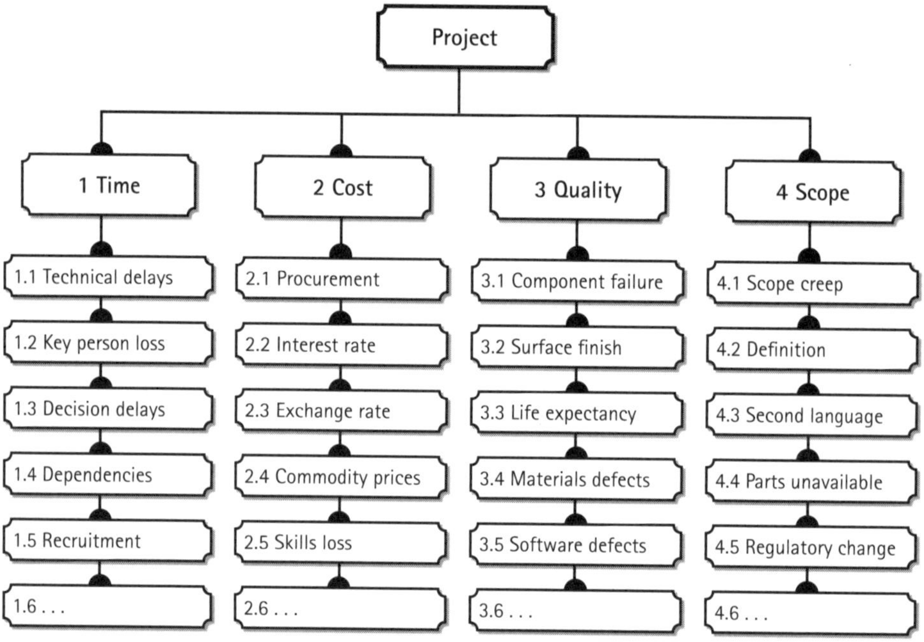

We will address some of the major risks shown in the example RBS in Figure 2.5.

PLANNING OUT SCOPE RISKS

One of the biggest risks projects face is "scope creep". This is the tendency for people to bundle additional work into your project and so get their objectives met using your budget, resources and effort. The danger of this is evident: in using your resources to meet my objectives, you will compromise your ability to meet your own objectives.

Planning Out Risk 15

The commonest cause of scope creep is not malice, stupidity or opportunism; it is simply confusion. If the boundary of your scope is not clearly delineated, I may assume that what I want is in scope, whilst you, with equal merit, assume it is out of scope. Defining the boundary with precision is a vital first step to fixing your scope and managing this aspect of risk.

To make your boundary as precise as possible, you must define not just what is in scope, but equally, what is out of scope. This requires you to use your experience – and that of your team – to foresee where scope misunderstandings are likely to occur.

Figure 2.6: Scope Creep and Defining Scope

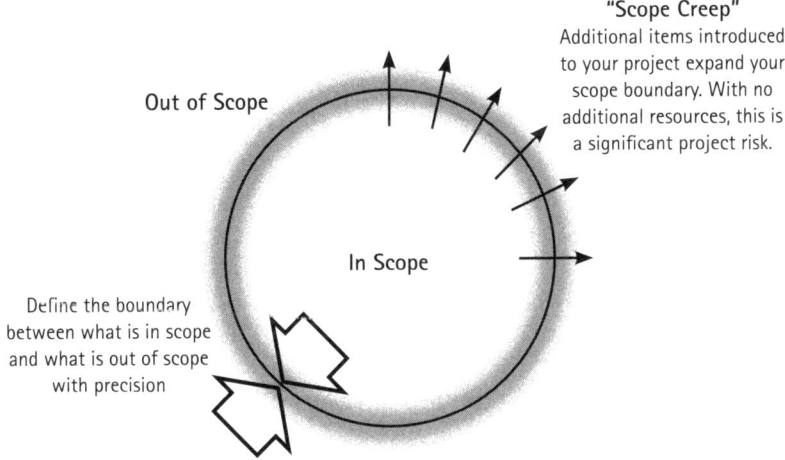

The second step is to get the precise definition of the project's scope signed off by your project sponsor, so that you have an authoritative voice supporting you when you resist pressures to expand the scope. With your scope defined, let us examine some powerful tools that will help you further manage scope risk: the Work Breakdown Structure (WBS), Product Breakdown Structure (PBS) and the RACI chart (see below).

Defining the Work and Deliverables

To move from a scope statement to a plan in your project definition, you will need to articulate your project activities and deliverables item-by-item. The tools that will allow you to do this are the WBS for setting out your activities, and the PBS for setting out your project deliverables, or products. Whichever you use is a matter partly of circumstance and partly of preference. It can also be the result of culture and training. In the United States, the Project Management Institute (PMI) uses the term WBS for a breakdown of products rather than activities. Projects that deliver complex assets are far more likely to benefit from a PBS, whilst organisational projects with few and simple physical deliverables will usually prefer a WBS.

Work Breakdown Structure (WBS)

Figure 2.7 illustrates a WBS for creating an opening ceremony for a new village hall. Here, it is the tasks that are represented in the boxes, and

Figure 2.7: Work Breakdown Structure

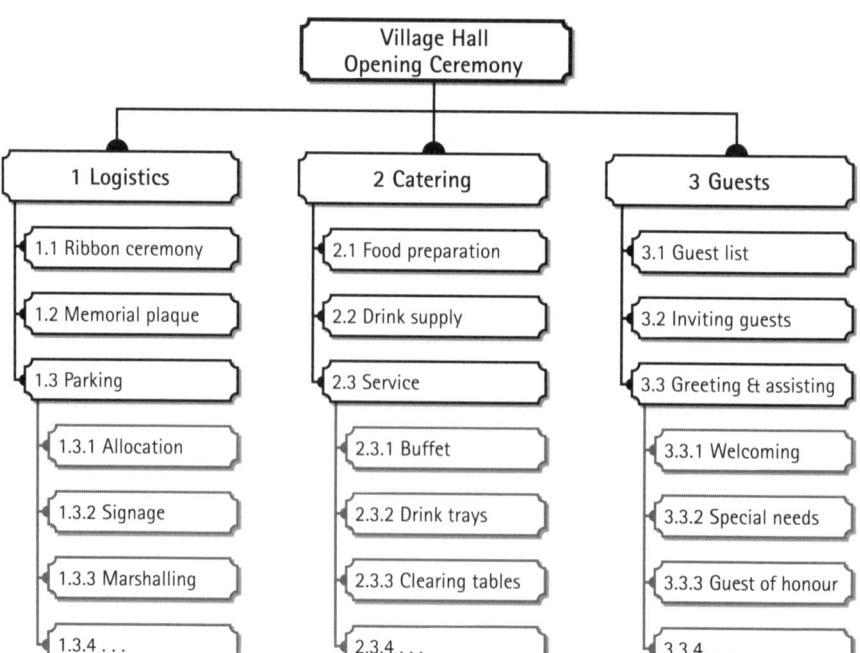

these can be allocated a cost to create a project budget, as well as people to do them, to create a project organisation chart. (We will see in Chapter 4 how you can use your WBS to identify specific project risks.)

Product Breakdown Structure (PBS)

Figure 2.8 shows an illustrative PBS for a project involving fitting a new kitchen. It shows how each component that has to be sourced or fabricated can be assigned a unique PBS number or product reference. This allows project managers to document specifications and quality standards for each product and track delivery, and sign-off against the standards.

Figure 2.8: Product Breakdown Structure

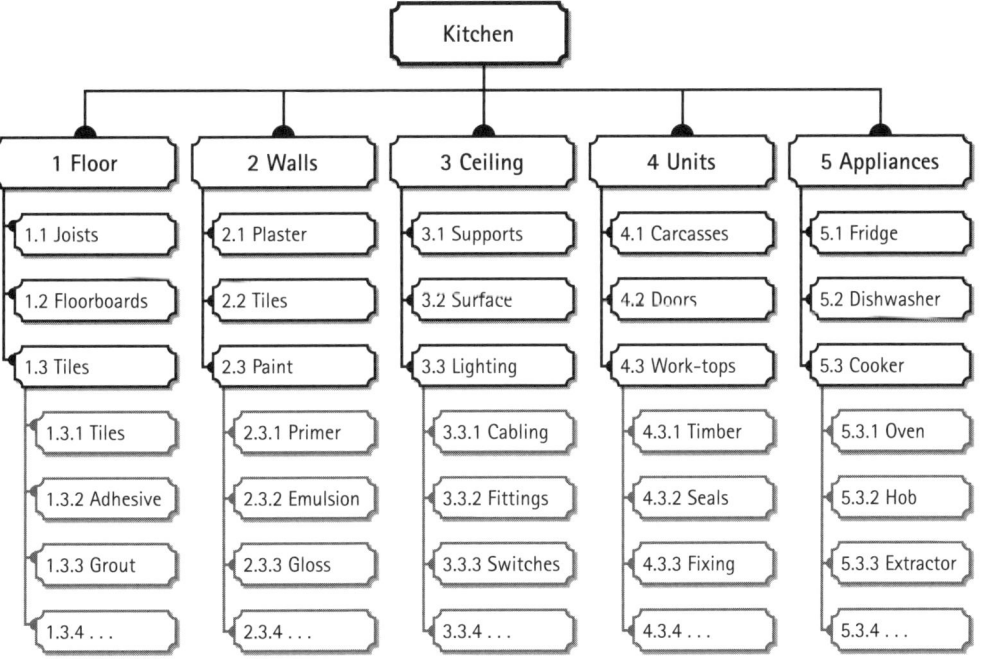

Assigning Ownership and Resources

One way to reduce scope risk is to ensure that people feel a sense of responsibility for the project. At the top of the project hierarchy will be your *sponsor*. This can be your boss, a senior person in your organisation, someone in a commissioning organisation, your client, your customer or your spouse! It is your sponsor who determines that the project is needed and is prepared to work to promote it on behalf of the interests they represent.

Other people have a stake in your project too; we call them *stakeholders* and they are crucial to the success of your project. So much so, in fact, that Chapter 10 is dedicated to them. Stakeholders have to be kept informed and often consulted about the scope of your project. Since you cannot please all of your stakeholders all of the time, determining your scope must involve negotiation. As with all negotiations, you will need to assess your stakeholders, evaluate their needs, and make decisions about who to please and who to disappoint.

A RACI chart is a useful tool for tracking stakeholders and recording how they will interact with elements of your scope. Figure 2.9 shows an example of how it can be used in our opening ceremony project.

Figure 2.9: RACI Chart

	Responsible	Authority	Consult	Inform
Logistics	Ian	Jon	Rotary Club Parish Council	Residents
Catering	Carol	Eileen	W.I. Parish Council	Local shops
Guests	Jon	Eileen	Rotary Club Parish Council	Councillor Residents

In the chart, Jon is the project manager, while Eileen is chair of the village committee and project sponsor. Ian and Carol are volunteers.

Controlling Changes to Scope

Freezing scope and never letting it change would be the dream of most project managers. However, things do change, and as your project progresses, you are likely to learn new information, as will your stakeholders. Freezing your scope and your specification is not a pragmatic solution and could often result in your project delivering products or services that are already out of date – particularly with longer projects.

However, a reckless acceptance of all requests to change the scope or specification of your project can lead to chaos.

> ❝*If project content is allowed to change freely, the rate of change will exceed the rate of progress.*❞
>
> Bill Brasington (the fifth of nine "Brasington's Laws" of project management)

At this stage, we need to acknowledge the need to control scope changes as a means of managing risk. We will examine how to do this in Chapter 9.

PLANNING OUT SCHEDULE RISKS

Failing to plan is tantamount to planning to fail, and this is particularly so when scheduling. Examples of projects that are delayed and run late are legion. Successfully planning a project schedule includes three elements:

1. **Tasks**

   We have already seen how your work breakdown structure will give you a comprehensive list of project activities.

2. **Dependencies**

   Some tasks can get done at any time and are independent of other activities. Others can only occur at specific times, linked to events like the start or completion of other tasks. These linkages are called dependencies.

3. **Durations**

   Durations measure how long each task is predicted to take. Whilst creating a full list of tasks is susceptible to rigorous thinking and checking, and identifying dependencies between those tasks is subject to logic and analysis, durations can only ever be estimates. Therefore, much schedule risk arises from planned durations of activities. Missed activities and unforeseen dependencies will also be significant contributing factors.

Types of Dependencies

Dependencies are logical links between activities. The commonest form of dependency, by far, is the "finish-to-start dependency". For example: you cannot start painting a wall until you have finished preparing it, and you cannot mash a potato until you have finished boiling it.

The next most common dependency is the "finish-to-finish dependency". Anyone who cooks will know that you don't cook the peas, then the carrots, then the potatoes, then put the joint of meat in the oven. Instead, you calculate when each needs to start cooking, based on how long it will take, and when you want the whole meal to be ready. Start-to-start and start-to-finish dependencies are much rarer.

Let's go back to our finish-to-start dependency for a moment and think about painting a wall. If the wall and the paint are sound, then to freshen up the wall, the only preparation you will need to do is to wash the wall thoroughly with sugar soap. As soon as you have washed it, you can paint the wall... Not quite. You will need to wait for an hour or so to let the walls dry thoroughly first.

You could treat this waiting time as a task, but since you could be doing another task at the same time, this hour is usually described as a "lag". We have a finish-to-start dependency with a 1 hour lag. The opposite of a lag is a "lead". If you want your roast beef to rest for 20 minutes before serving it at 1 p.m., then the relationship with the timing for the roast potatoes, which are due to come out of the oven at 12:55, is a finish-to-finish dependency with a 15 minute lead.

Planning your schedule begins with identifying the dependencies between tasks. Take time to do this thoroughly and get somebody to check your logic, because your whole project schedule will depend on getting this right.

Estimating Durations

The first step in estimating durations (and, indeed, estimating costs) is to review everything you know about the technical solution and deliverables. An important component of this will be the records and personal experiences of previous projects with similar deliverables, constraints and other characteristics. What were the actual times that activities took and what were the challenges the project teams faced? Organisational learning is a vital part of risk management and we will look at it in more depth in Chapter 13.

Estimating Techniques

Table 2.1 shows the main estimating techniques that you can use. Use more than one approach and look for ways to understand any discrepancies between your independent estimates. Wide variations of estimate mean high risk. If you can test your assumptions and refine your logic to the point where different people get similar estimates through different processes, you will have achieved a lot in terms of risk reduction.

Table 2.1: Estimating Techniques	
Rules of thumb	Simple guidelines that have been developed from years of experience.
Formal estimating methodologies	Some projects working in mature development areas like the software, pharmaceutical and construction industries have formal methodologies for estimating process times.
Bottom-up estimating	In disciplines where the estimator has experience of the type of project, bottom-up estimating is an effective way to build up a project schedule one activity at a time. It is best done from a work breakdown structure.
Multiple broad brush estimates	Where you have little or no experience, two or more independent estimates are important, to give some level of confidence. Where the estimates differ, explore the different assumptions and approaches to learn from them.
The Delphi Technique	This is a formal version of the above approach. Estimators can use any approach they choose, and results and reasoning are collated and presented anonymously to all estimators. Revised estimates are then prepared and the cycle repeats until either you get a narrow range of estimates or a major difference in understanding emerges, which you can investigate.
Outside experts and consultants	Where you do not have the experience to create a credible schedule, bring in people who do. *more >>>*

Back of the envelope	In any non-trivial project, you should always review the estimate for "common sense". Do the assumptions seem reasonable? Are there any arithmetical errors? Does the final estimate seem about right? If not, is the reason for this apparent?
Compare bottom-up and top-down estimates	These will differ – often materially. You can learn a lot when you understand where and why. What have you learned about your assumptions (or arithmetic!)?

Errors and Omissions

Table 2.2 offers you some reminders of common project estimating errors and omissions. To help you ensure that you have dealt with all of these variables make sure that all of your assumptions are fully documented and are tested where possible.

Table 2.2: Common Estimating Errors and Omissions

Errors
- Underestimating the time and cost of management and administration.
- Underestimating the time and cost of maintaining tools and equipment during development.
- Underestimating the time and cost of familiarisation for the project team.
- Underestimating the time and cost of scope creep and redefinition of the specification.
- Underestimating the time and cost of user training and support.
- Underestimating the time and cost of integrating new products, systems or services with existing ones.
- Underestimating the time and cost of designing tests, preparing or acquiring test data, testing and fixing the faults.
- Believing that there won't be any faults.
- Don't forget to check your arithmetic... twice.

Omissions
- Project management overhead – the time it takes to plan, monitor and control your project, and manage the team of people. A range of 10–25% is typical.
- Change management – building "stuff" is often the easy part. Working with people to win acceptance of changes is extremely time-consuming and resource intensive.
- Holidays, illness and other commitments create dead time when people are unable to make progress on your project. Build these in or allow sufficient contingency.
- Sensitivity analysis and confidence levels are an essential part of your estimate. Without them, it is just a guess – lucky or not. There is a real difference between: "We expect this task to be completed in 12 weeks", and "Our best estimate is 12 weeks and we are 90% confident that it will take between 11 and 14 weeks". The latter is a far more credible and useful estimate for risk management.
- Training, familiarisation and induction all take time, cost money and need resources.
- Purchase or hire of any accommodation, specialised tools or other equipment.
- Relationship management overheads – when you are using contractors, subcontractors or consultants of any sort, or working with partners, what is your commitment to managing the relationship and what does it involve?
- Preparing the final report.

Three-Point Estimates

There are many alternative sources of information about formal project estimating, such as the Programme Evaluation and Review Technique (PERT). However, it is useful to introduce it briefly. PERT uses what are called "three-point estimates". These start with a "most likely" estimate of duration, labelled B in Figure 2.10. To this you would add an "optimistic estimate" of the shortest likely duration (A) and a "pessimistic estimate" of the longest likely duration (C).

Figure 2.10: PERT Estimates

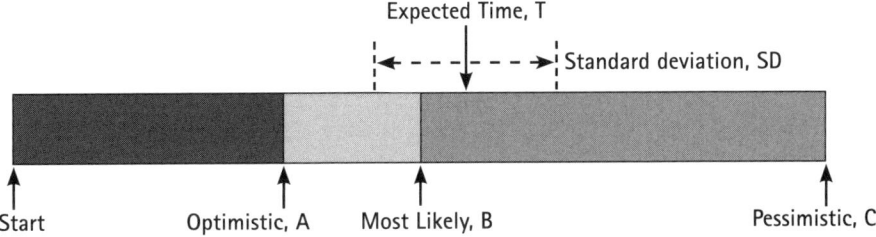

Based on statistical mathematics, PERT gives us an estimate of the "expected time", or T, from a very straightforward calculation:

$$\text{Expected Time, T} = \frac{A + 4 \times B + C}{6}$$

PERT also gives us a way to estimate the confidence limits for this expected time, called the "standard deviation", or SD. We would express the duration as T ± SD.

$$\text{Standard Deviation, SD} = \frac{C - A}{6}$$

It is important to remember that these three point estimates appear more reliable than they are. The use of mathematical equations can give the illusion of "science", but all we are doing is replacing one estimate with three, and your "most likely" estimate is still subject to the same errors and omissions as any other.

PLANNING IN CONTINGENCY

Don't believe your estimate! You will make estimating mistakes, so you will need a contingency. Set it to be consistent with the confidence level attached to your estimate and the level of project risk. In any but the most familiar type of project consider a contingency in the range 15–30%, or even higher for a highly novel project. This will increase your base cost but increase your confidence of delivering within your planned margins of error.

We discussed finish-to-start dependencies above and it is these that give rise to characteristic sequences of one activity following another. These sequences carry much of our schedule risk. If one activity slips, then the next must start late. But if the late start means one of the people who need to be involved is unavailable, then not only will this activity end late due to the late start, it may, itself, take longer. This can lead to ever increasing slippage. Sound familiar?

Figure 2.11: Slippage in highly dependent tasks

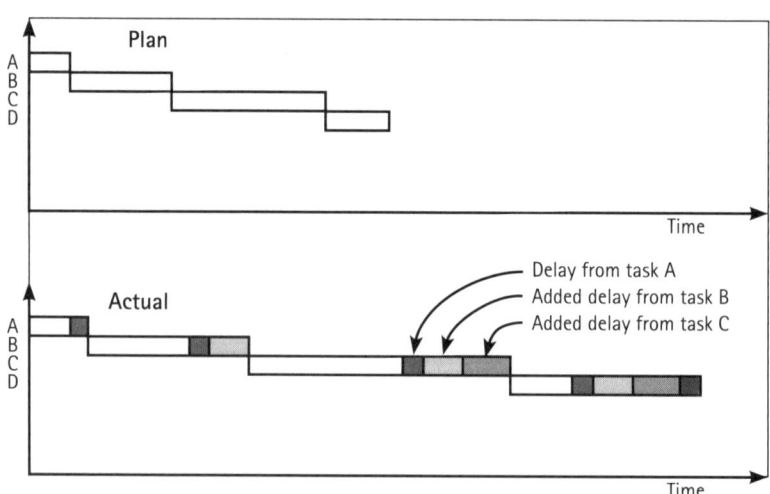

This complexity is one of the largest sources of project risk, so project managers have found a way to contain the risk. The method has been used by project managers for many years – probably centuries – but in the 1990s it came to be known as the Critical Chain Method (CCM). The principle is much like the way fire crews handle vast fires in woodland or even (more rarely) in cities. They hack down trees in the path of the fire to create a void large enough to prevent the fire crossing it. The fire burns itself out.

We can do the same with schedule risk by allowing a contingency period at the end of a sequence of dependent tasks before the next task is scheduled to begin. Building in an artificial lag in this way creates an "island of stability" in your project, where accumulated slippage can be absorbed and the project team can use any spare time to catch up with admin and discretionary tasks before the next sequence of activities begins.

Figure 2.12: Islands of stability in a project schedule

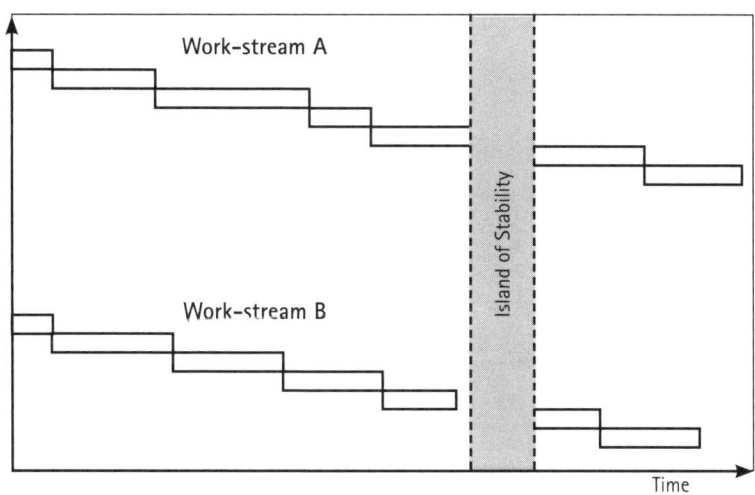

Planning Out Cost and Resource Risks

Much of the estimating guidance in the last section applies equally when estimating budget and resource requirements. In this section, we will look at a specific bottom-up way to estimate resource and budget requirements using your Work Breakdown Structure (WBS) and then go on to examine two particular resource risks: allocation and capability.

Costing and Resourcing your WBS

Once you have a WBS for your project, the simplest way to create a budget is to start at the lowest level (the smallest tasks) and for each task, estimate a cost. You can then add these up to create an estimate for the work packages at the next level. Repeat this through all of the levels and the final figure you get at the top will be your estimated project cost. You now have a Cost Breakdown Structure, or CBS.

You can add contingency at any level. You could, for example, add a single contingency sum for the whole project. This has the merit of simplicity, but the weakness that it may be too simple. You could add contingency to each of the major groups of task at the top level, called work streams. This allows you to add a greater or lesser contingency according to your confidence in the estimates. Some of these work streams will be more familiar and straightforward: others more risky. At the other extreme, you could allocate a contingency sum to each activity at the bottom level.

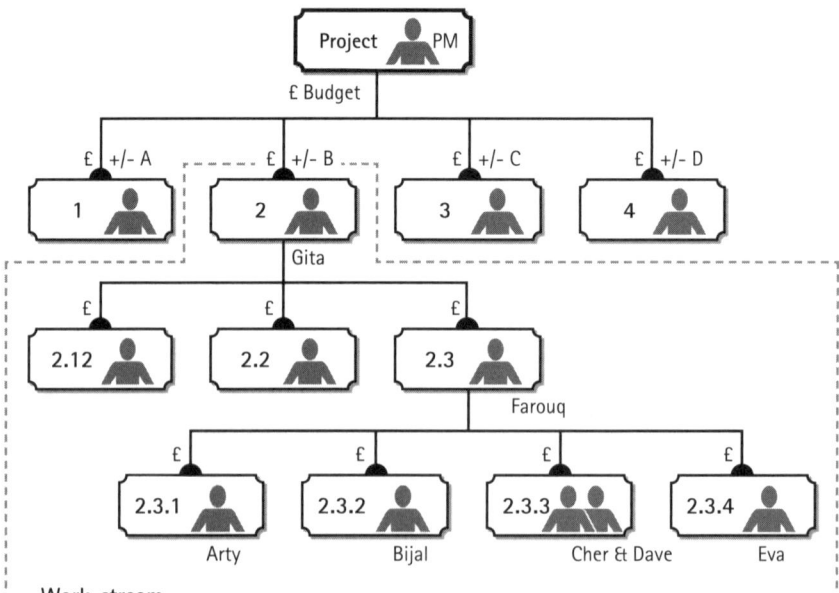

Figure 2.13: Cost and Organisational Breakdown Structure

An effective way to add contingency (see Figure 2.13) is to add contingency at the level at which the budget will be managed. In this case, the budget is managed as "work stream leaders". Figure 2.13 also illustrates a useful way to apply resources to your plan, by allocating the individuals with the right skills and experience to each task, and then adding the supervisory team members and work stream leaders. You now have an Organisational Breakdown Structure, or OBS.

Allocating Workload

Have you ever noticed how some people seem to attract massive workloads and struggle purposefully to discharge them, while others are virtually overlooked? There are often good reasons for this in the mind of the person who makes the allocation: "Chris is such a good worker"; or "Sam isn't ready for this kind of responsibility."

The risk here is that some people get overloaded while others get bored. Neither is good for morale and long term effectiveness, and overloading someone can lead to catastrophic failure. An important aspect of risk-based planning is to spread the workload as evenly as skills and experience allows.

It also pays to make sure there is slack in your resourcing and that no team member is scheduled to full capacity. That would lead to slippage. When project sponsor Brian pushed his project manager to schedule staff to work on the project at weekends to get the project done more quickly, his project manager rightly argued against it. Brian thought that the reason was one of care for staff or unwillingness to take the tough decisions. Whilst the project manager did care for the staff, he also knew that if they were scheduled to work at weekends and a problem arose, there would be no contingency time available to absorb the extra work, and the project would be forced to deliver late.

Right People – Right Skills

Having the best people available is a joy. However, life is seldom so accommodating, so it pays to survey the skills required for the project and the skills you actually have available to you. Analyse the gap and make a plan for how to bridge it with coaching, training, support, contract staff or additional learning time. This is an important part of your risk management plan.

PLANNING OUT QUALITY RISKS

A major source of delay in projects is due to the failure of a client to accept handover of the project deliverables, because they do not meet specification. And a frighteningly common reason that the deliverables do not meet specifications is that there either are no specifications or they are imprecise. So, now the client can interpret them in the way that suits them today, whilst the project manager interpreted them as they appeared in the planning stage of the project. Lesson: take the time needed to negotiate and develop detailed specifications, and then get them signed off as binding, subject to a formal change control process.

Assuming you have done this, there are three quality processes to build into your project, to manage the risk that your deliverables do not meet the approved standard.

The Three Quality Processes

1. **Quality Design (QD)**
   From the outset, establish the right level of quality for each deliverable (which should never be "perfect"). Design your deliverables to explicitly meet this standard and ensure that the sign off of your specifications explicitly acknowledges that the designed quality level is right for the purpose.

2. **Quality Control (QC)**
   This is the process that checks to ensure that the quality standards have been met. It is fundamentally an oversight process. Your QC process should also include procedures for how you will address shortcomings in the delivered products.

3. **Quality Assurance (QA)**
   This is the process that keeps a focus on getting the quality right and can be subject to internal, national or international standards – some of which are specific to particular industries. Make no mistake, however: a written process is valuable, but the soul of a QA process is the culture of the team that is working together.

Support all of these processes with a *Quality Plan*. For each project, this will show how each process will operate, what resources will be available and who has responsibility for each aspect.

CHAPTER 3
THE RISK MANAGEMENT PROCESS

RISK IS ABOUT UNCERTAINTY, and in the face of uncertainty, there is one thing you can rely on to help you: a good process. A good process is one that brings repeatable results that meet your needs. It should be as simple as possible, but not more simple than necessary. Simplicity makes it easy to remember and easy to follow day-to-day, under the pressure of events. If you have in place a good process: trust it. Follow it, persevere with it, and you will get good results.

This chapter introduces a simple and effective process for managing project risk. You will see how four steps are all that you need for a scalable process that does everything you want. You will also find out how to adapt the process to circumstances. We will also look at the roles and responsibilities that go with project risk management and how to document your project risk plan.

Figure 3.1: The Risk Management Process

```
┌─────────────────────────────────────┐
│         ┌──────────┐                │
│         │ Identify │                │
│         └────┬─────┘                │
│              ⇩                      │
│         ┌──────────┐ ⇐──┐           │
│         │ Analyse  │    │           │
│         └────┬─────┘    │           │
│              ⇩       Monitor        │
│         ┌──────────┐   and          │
│         │   Plan   │  Control       │
│         └────┬─────┘    │           │
│              ⇩          │           │
│         ┌──────────┐ ───┘           │
│         │  Action  │                │
│         └──────────┘                │
│      Risk Management Framework      │
└─────────────────────────────────────┘
```

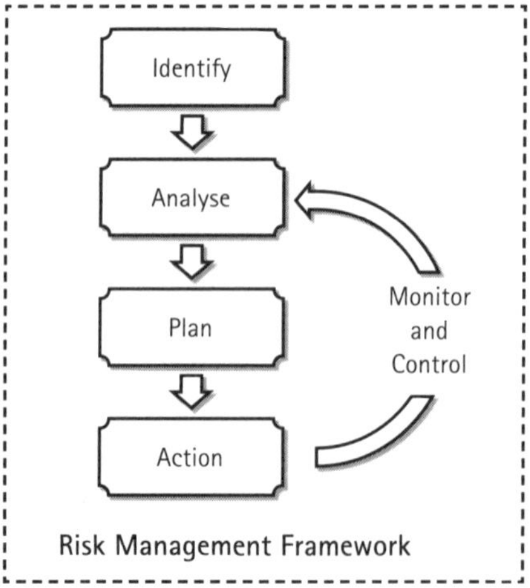

THE FUNDAMENTAL RISK MANAGEMENT PROCESS

Figure 3.1 illustrates the four steps in managing project risk, and the review process. We will examine each of these in turn.

- **Identify**
  You can do nothing until you know what your risks are, so the first step is to identify the threats and opportunities your project faces. Chapter 4 covers this step in more detail.
- **Analyse**
  Once you have identified your risks, you need to understand them. Chapter 5 will give you the tools you need to assess your risks, considering them both qualitatively and quantitatively.
- **Plan**
  Once you understand your risks, you need to put together a plan. In Chapter 6, you will learn the six fundamental risk management strategies that will form the basis of your response to every threat.
- **Action**
  Planning is all very well, but unless you take action, nothing will change. Chapter 7 offers a daily routine for managing your risks actively.

Monitor and Control

These four steps will only work if you persevere. You must constantly review what is happening on your project and analyse what you are learning. Did you get the result you expected from your action? If you did, that's great. If you did not, then you need to examine why not, make a new plan and take further action. This is the "monitor and control" loop for risk management and it is the secret of success. Thomas Edison said: "Genius is one per cent inspiration: ninety-nine per cent perspiration", and the same is true of project success. It is your commitment to persevere that will give you real control over risks. This will be covered in Chapter 8. Simple does not mean the same as easy: the process is simple, but remaining committed to it, and doing it well, is far from easy.

Why Only Five Parts?

There are many books and manuals that describe their own risk management process and many of them are listed in the *Learn More* appendices at the back of this book. In those sources, you will find anything from four to nine steps. None of those processes contains anything that is not included in our five-step framework. (The advantage of five steps is that it is easy to remember.)

Psychologist George A. Miller researched how many items in a list a typical adult could recall. He found considerable variation, but a distinct average at around seven. Most people were able to recall between five and nine objects. So to give you the best possible chance of being able to recall this process when it really matters, here are the five things you need to remember:

Identify – Analyse – Plan – Action – Review

SCALING THE FUNDAMENTAL PROCESS

You can adapt this fundamental process to the most straightforward or the most complex projects. First, you need to understand what your project needs and the environment it sits within.

Drivers for Scale and Complexity

At the simplest level, you can hold a short meeting to identify project risks, assess their relative importance, put together a prioritised plan of action and carry it out; then observe your project for new risks. This need only take a little time; and, on a small project, such an approach will be entirely satisfactory. On a large-scale, challenging project, the identification may involve teams of experts and be followed by detailed analysis and quantitative modelling that drives decisions about your project's programme. Detailed plans for many of the potential risks will look like full project plans in their own right, and teams will be tasked with delivering them. The constant monitoring and reporting of risk status will involve formal reports and daily meetings.

Table 3.1 lists some of the ways that you can adapt the fundamental process to the needs of your project and the environment within which you are pursuing it.

Table 3.1: Variables of Scale and Complexity for Your Risk Management Process

Investment in the process	• Budget for risk management processes and activities • Number of people involved • Seniority of the people involved
Degree of formality	• Amount of documentation required • Depth and detail of documentation • Hierarchy and role descriptions of people involved
Methodologies used	• Choice of techniques and tools used • Number of analytical tools used • Use or not of quantitative analysis methods
Level of detail	• Level of threat considered high priority • Detail of risk planning • Frequency of monitoring, reviewing and audits

Table 3.2 lists some of the factors that will influence your decision about how to scale the risk management process. In Chapter 4, we will explore the Project Risk Potential Review. This is a formal tool that will help you gauge the level of risk your project carries and can help you when deciding on scaling the risk management process.

Table 3.2: Drivers of Scale and Complexity for Your Risk Management Process

Scale of project	• Absolute size of project in terms of investment, resources involved, duration, or impact on its sponsoring organisation or its community • Relative size of the project in the context of its sponsoring organisation or its community
Level of threat	• Cost at risk • Implications of failure or delay • Significance to its sponsoring organisation or its community • Reputational risk
Uncertainty of outcome	• Level of novelty of the project, use of new or untried solutions, or innovation required to deliver the outcome • Experience and maturity of project management within the team that is delivering it • Changeability of external factors such as political or social pressures
Prevailing environment	• Degree of oversight and effectiveness of existing governance processes • Culture of the sponsoring organisation • Levels of resilience and optimism

ROLES AND RESPONSIBILITIES

A process can only be effective if people take responsibility for implementing it. There are no universal role descriptions for project management and risk management roles, so the most valuable thing will be for you to take time to draw up a set of "role descriptions" or "terms of reference" that will work for your project. To do this, consider what your project needs, the prevailing culture within your organisation and the characters of the individuals concerned.

To help stimulate your thinking, Table 3.3 sets out some sample roles and responsibilities that you can adapt to your own situation.

Table 3.3: Sample Roles and Responsibilities for Project Risk Management	
Project Sponsor	*Also known as project director (or in the UK public sector, as senior responsible owner, or SRO), the project sponsor acts to promote the project at senior levels, supports and guides the project manager, provides oversight of the project, and makes high level decisions.* In risk management, the project sponsor's roles and responsibilities typically include: • Ensuring that the project is fully defined and that the definitions of goal, objectives and scope are signed off • Reviewing and signing-off the risk management process and the risk management plan • Being the point of escalation for major project issues • Making risk response and risk investment decisions that exceed the project manager's authority • Securing the resources and budget needed for the process and for individual risk responses • Acting as a critical friend to the project manager to ensure that the risk management process is being followed conscientiously • Acting as authority for changes to project scope or functionality, under formal change control
Project Board	*Sometimes also known as a steering group, the project board's role is dependent on the governance arrangements of its organisation. Most typically, it is the ultimate project decision maker and has a role in overseeing the project and holding its officers to account. In the UK public sector, where the SRO has ultimate responsibility, the board should be an advisory body to support the SRO; but even here, it often will out-rank the SRO and make the final decisions on the most substantive matters.* *more >>>*

The Risk Management Process

Project Board (cont'd)	With regards to risk management, the project board's roles and responsibilities typically include: • Determining the thresholds for the project's appetite for risk – what levels of risk will and will not be tolerable to the organisation • Overall strategic decisions within the business or organisational context, including the go/no-go decision for the project at project gateways • Implementing project governance frameworks and promotion of good project governance • Owning strategic level project risks that can affect the whole organisation • Being the ultimate point of escalation for all decisions • Strategic oversight of the project and its risk register • May act as authority for changes to project scope or functionality, under formal change control • Receiving final project report and lessons learned document and responsible for relaying these to the wider organisation • Approving final project closure
Project Manager	*The project manager has day-to-day responsibility for all aspects of delivering the project, from budget to people management, planning to reporting, rapid response to sign-off.* With respect to risk management, the project manager's roles and responsibilities typically include: • Establishing a risk management process and documenting a risk management plan • Ownership and maintenance of the risk register • Driving or assigning responsibility for the risk management process • Determining thresholds for what levels of risk will and will not be tolerable to the project • Signing off risk response plans and ensuring single point responsibilities are allocated • Managing relationships with stakeholders and ensuring their perspectives feed into the risk management process • Active monitoring and control of the project to ensure new threats and opportunities are noted and managed • Making day-to-day decisions on the management of risks and issues, including minor budgetary and change control decisions (the term "minor" will need to be carefully defined for your project) • Overseeing the risk management activities of consultants, contractors and partners • Reporting on risks and issues to the project sponsor and project board • Engaging constructively with the project audit process • Escalating risks to the project sponsor or project board, as appropriate • Encouraging the project sponsor and project board to engage positively with the risk management process • On-going evaluation of the risk management process and risk management plan, and making changes as necessary • Preparing a final report on lessons learned On a larger project, the project manager may delegate some of these roles. <div align="right">*more >>>*</div>

Risk Manager	Sometimes known as a risk champion, the risk manager will only have a role on a large project, where the project manager delegates their authority for day-to-day risk management. Where the project has a full-time or part-time risk manager, it is essential to document the level of authority and responsibilities that the project manager has delegated.
	The risk manager's roles and responsibilities typically include: • Preparing the risk management plan • Creating, maintaining and monitoring the risk register • Conducting detailed risk analysis • Allocating responsibility for individual risks to risk owners (see below) • Preparing and presenting project risk reports • Designing, facilitating and documenting risk workshops • Engaging constructively with the risk management audit process (see Chapter 8) • Being a source of risk management expertise and good practice to the whole project team • Advising the project manager and project sponsor on all aspect of risk management
Risk Owner	The risk owner is responsible for the management of a single risk within the project.
	The risk owner's roles and responsibilities typically include: • Describing the risk formally • Identifying management options and selecting the most cost-effective • Developing and documenting a Risk Action Plan (RAP) • Ensuring that the RAP is carried out • Monitoring and reviewing the outcomes of the RAP • Providing status updates on the risk to feed into the risk register • Making a recommendation that a risk can be closed in the risk register The risk owner may appoint one or more people to carry out actions within the RAP.
Project Audit, or Project Risk Audit	Also known as an external risk review or project review, an audit reviews the process and the way decisions are made, rather than the decisions themselves. It provides the organisation with assurance that the project is being run effectively and accountably and ensures that the risk management process is being run effectively.
	The auditor's roles and responsibilities typically include: • Evaluating the process and role descriptions • Sampling risk register entries and examining them in depth • Reviewing risk management documentation • Questioning the key participants in the risk process (see above) • Providing challenge and recommendations to improve risk management practices Chapter 8 includes a more detailed look at the wider topic of project assurance.

What is most important is not that you apply these roles and definitions, but that that you identify the roles that you need for your project and document clear responsibilities for each. Also remember that this table is limited to the risk management components of each role.

RISK MANAGEMENT PLAN

An important part of your risk management process will be the documentation that supports it. Figure 3.2 illustrates the typical range of risk management documents that may be used on a larger project. We have already seen how you can scale your process to the needs of your project, so do not be alarmed if this seems like a lot of paperwork!

Figure 3.2: Core Risk Management Documents

- Risk Management Plan
- Schedule of Risks
- Risk Register / Risk Analysis
- Risk Action Plans / Contingency Plans / Business Continuity Plans
- Risk Reports / Lessons Learned

Risk Management Framework: Identify → Analyse → Plan → Action

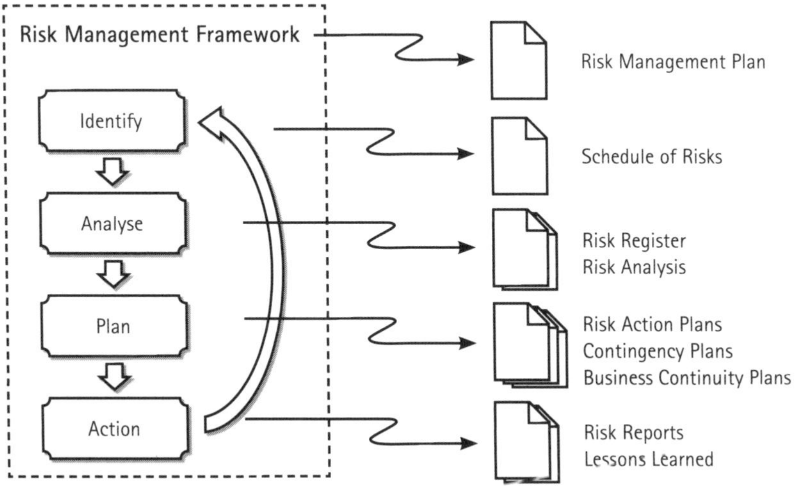

"Project management: it's all just bureaucracy and paperwork."

"It's all just bureaucracy and paperwork" is a frequent lament. And it can be – if you let it. So, follow Mike's rule number 1 – only fill in a form or complete a template if either:
- it helps you achieve your project objective, or
- it is necessary to support accountability and good governance.

Having said that, there are many good reasons for documenting aspects of your risk management process, some of which are set out in Table 3.4 below.

Table 3.4: Reasons for Documenting Your Risk Management Process

- Creates a record and an audit trail of plans, decisions and actions
- Gives everyone a common understanding of your process, and therefore leads to consistency in the actions they take
- Helps prompt and clarify your thinking
- Communicates plans, processes and actions to team members
- Standard templates ensure components do not get missed
- Useful basis for later lessons learned, and an archive for organisational knowledge management

Putting Together a Risk Management Plan

We will examine each of the documents in Figure 3.2 at the appropriate stage of the book. We will begin with the risk management plan. You can download a *Risk Happens!* template for a risk management plan from *www.riskhappens.co.uk* or you can build your own to meet your project's needs. Table 3.5 sets out the topics that a risk management plan would typically cover.

Table 3.5: Typical Contents of a Risk Management Plan

Introduction	• Importance of risk management to the project • Executive summary • Overview of contents
Background	• Organisational context • Project definition
Risk context	• Overall assessment of project risk • Organisational appetite for risk and risk tolerance
Risk management process	• Process steps and titles; reference to a process guide • Risk management documentation, with samples in appendices • Roles and responsibilities • Levels of authority and delegation • Risk review guidelines or procedures
Methodologies to be used	• Risk identification tools • Risk analysis tools • Selection criteria • Definitions of scales for risk likelihoods, impacts and proximities

more >>>

| Project controls | - Quality control, quality assurance, reference to a quality plan
- Change control
- Supplier, contractor and consultant management processes |
|---|---|
| Stakeholders | - Communication plan
- Reporting cycle and templates |
| Other information | - Schedule of key risk management dates
- Risk management audit requirements
- Risk breakdown structure
- Budget for risk management
- Project risk management glossary |

CHAPTER 4
IDENTIFY RISKS

THIS CHAPTER WILL GIVE YOU the tools you need to help you to identify project risks. We begin by surveying the whole project, then describe six basic approaches to finding risks, and some tools for each approach. The chapter ends with an introduction to the project manager's most fundamental and important risk management tool: the risk register.

Identifying risk is about detecting uncertainties and assumptions. In carrying out this search, there are three questions to ask, each representing a different way of viewing the world:
- What could go wrong?
- What don't we know?
- What assumptions have we made?

So, for example, "the second round of funding for our project could be cut back" is equivalent to "we do not know how the second round of funding will be allocated"; which amounts to the same as "we have assumed that the second round of funding will be available; but it may not be". There is nothing wrong with making assumptions – we have to if we want to progress the project at all. The error comes when we fail to acknowledge that a strongly-held belief is just an assumption. Each assumption contains a risk: it may be wrong.

Right from the start of your project, all risks – even where not quantifiable – should be identified and noted. It is important to re-visit this process periodically. Think about the right times or frequency with which to do so for your specific project – these may be at key milestones or at team meetings.

Figure 4.1: Periodic review to identify new risks

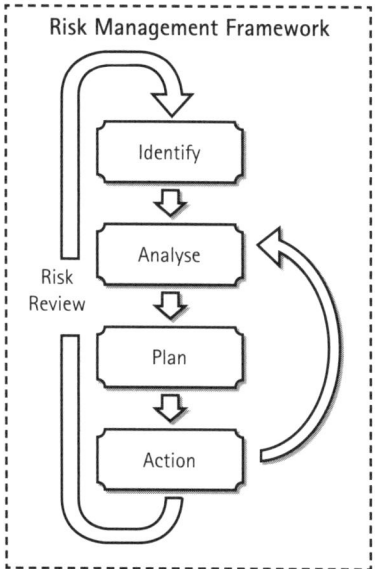

CONTEXT AND OBJECTIVES

There are two places to start when looking for risks. Your project definition sets out its goal, objectives and scope, so these should strongly indicate some of the areas of fundamental risk to your project. Projects are not done in isolation: one objective may present a low risk to your organisation and a high risk to mine. So you should also factor in the context of your project. Figure 4.2 illustrates this.

Figure 4.2 shows the interactions between the project, its immediate organisational environment, and its wider external context. Considering these factors should lead you to identify threats and opportunities for your project; most important of all, it will provide stimulus for your kick-off workshop and the formal processes of risk identification.

In passing, it is worth noting that this review will also inform the start of two other risk management processes.

Figure 4.2: Starting place for identifying project risks

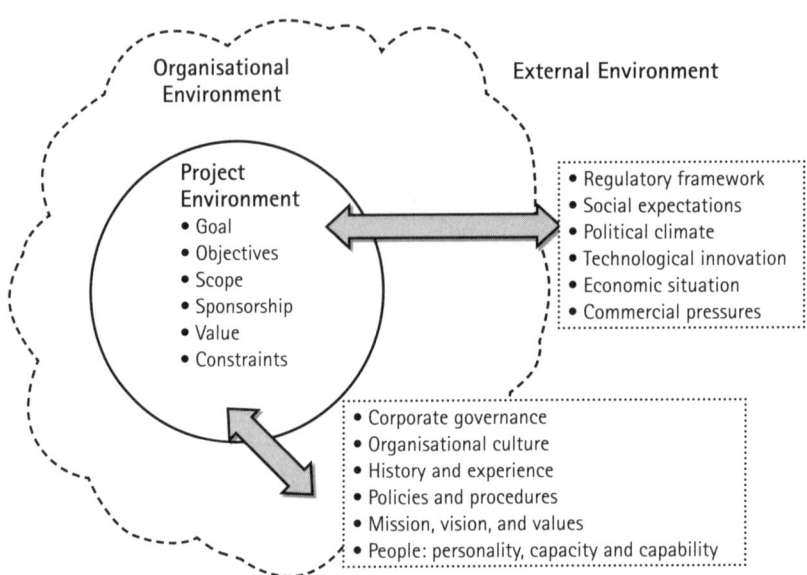

Stakeholder Management

Reviewing the organisational and external contexts of your project is also your starting point for identifying stakeholders, and therefore to your whole stakeholder management process (which is the subject of Chapter 10).

Setting the Red Zone

You should also consider your appetite for risk and set the level at which risks become intolerable (this is covered in more detail in Chapter 11). You must be prepared to terminate your project if the level of threat cannot be reduced. This is sometimes called "the red zone".

BEGIN WITH WHAT YOU DO AND DON'T KNOW

As you move towards a thorough review of your project, summon up all of the documentation and search it for likely sources of risk: missing or mistrusted information, vague or qualified statements, imposed constraints, inconsistencies, or assumptions that may be explicit or, more dangerous, positive statements that lack a sound base of evidence. Table 4.1 lists some of the core documents you will want to consider. Some of these will not have been prepared at the earlier stages of your project, so you will introduce these into later risk reviews.

Table 4.1: Core Project Documents	
Project definition and planning documents	• Project brief, or definition • Scope statement • Work and product breakdown structures • Resource plans and budget documents • Project schedule
Organisational references	• Project management process • Risk management policy • "Lessons learned documents" • Procurement procedures • Previous projects' risk registers

Revisit Time, Cost, Quality and Scope

In Chapter 2 we discussed planning out risk from the outset. At the heart of your project definition will be your objectives – most often in terms of time-schedule, cost-resources, quality-specification and scope-deliverables. Re-examine these to assess which ones ring alarm bells in your head or your team members'.

Risk Potential Review

You may want to consider a formal Risk Potential Review (RPR). This is a structured analysis of different aspects of your project that will give you an overall measure of the risk involved. In principle, you would expect a bigger, more cutting edge, more business critical, more politically sensitive project to carry more risk than a small, familiar, incremental, operational project.

An RPR is a structured set of questions that organisations develop to help assess the level of project risk. They use it to inform decisions about:
- which projects to undertake and which to abandon, defer or modify
- the level of process formality, governance and oversight a project requires.

Table 4.2 sets out some of the questions an RPR will typically address. If your organisation frequently considers project activity, it is worth creating a simple RPR questionnaire that is tailored to your needs.

Table 4.2: Typical Considerations for a Risk Potential Review	
Sponsorship	• Who is promoting the project? • What is their level of seniority? • Who is supporting the project?
Requirements	• What is driving the need for the project? • What is the strategic importance of the project? • What are the benefits? • What are the legislative/regulatory drivers? • How clearly are the requirements understood? • How fixed or changing are the requirements?
Scale of the project	• What is the proposed budget? (Expressed in absolute terms, or as a percentage of revenue or overall projects budget.) • What is the expected duration? • How complex is the project? • Which parts of the organisation will the project affect? (For example: all, several divisions, one division, one team.) • How many people are likely to be affected? (Expressed in absolute terms, or as a percentage of staff.) • How significant is the change that this project will introduce?
Impacts	• What is the potential impact on operational processes? • What is the potential impact on business as usual? • What is the potential impact on suppliers? • What is the potential impact on customers? • What is the potential impact on partners?
Constraints	• What are the legislative/regulatory requirements on the project? • What are the other constraints on this project? • Are there any accommodation constraints? • Are there any equipment, materiel or asset constraints?
Dependencies	• What internal teams/departments is the project dependent on? • What outside organisations is the project dependent on? • Is the project dependent on external events? • To what extent are we reliant on external suppliers or consultants? • What is the level of contractual complexity?
Capacity and capability	• Do we have the skills in house? • Do we have the numbers of people available that we need? • To what extent is the work familiar – do we understand this project? • To what extent do we have a track record with this kind of project? • Is there a strong market availability for the materials and services we will need? • Is the market experienced in supporting this kind of project?

more >>>

Novelty	• How familiar are we with this kind of project? • How familiar are we with this scale of project? • To what extent will this project rely on novel technologies? • To what extent will this project develop novel technologies?
Stakeholders	• How much work has been done on stakeholder analysis? • What level of stakeholder support has been achieved for the project? • What level of stakeholder opposition has been identified?

Against the answer to each of these questions, you would assign a threat level. With so many questions, a simple high–low–none assignment is likely to suffice. By allocating scores to these levels (2 for high, 1 for low, 0 for none) and adding them up, you can quickly achieve a simple numerical assessment of the level of potential risk for your project.

RISK KICK-OFF WORKSHOP

As soon as you have a project team available, consider running a "risk kick-off workshop". At the very least, include a session on risk as part of your "project kick off workshop". Getting eager minds around the problem of identifying and understanding project risks is the best way to kick-start risk management and is also a splendid way to begin developing a great team. In psychologist Bruce Tuckman's model of team formation, a new team needs a simple task that everybody can contribute to. Risk identification is a perfect way of bringing a team together.

In the next part of this chapter we will lay out six basic approaches your team can use. For now, let's look at how to set up your introductory workshop. You will also be able to adapt this structure to periodic risk review workshops, which could be either free-standing or a part of your regular project team meetings.

Workshop Agenda

Table 4.3 offers a sample risk workshop agenda, which goes beyond identification and into analysis and allocation of risk owners. Use this as your starting point and adapt it to the requirements of your project. This could be anything from an hour's session to a two-day workshop (which one author advocates). Use your instinct and the outcome of your Risk Potential Review (RPR) to guide you in determining how much time you should allocate.

It may be necessary to build a business case to justify the time and commitment you are proposing. If this is so, then a documented RPR will be a valuable asset.

Table 4.3: Indicative Risk Kick-off Workshop Agenda	
Introductions	You may or may not be a fan of ice-breakers, but you must certainly ensure everybody in the workshop is introduced to somebody else. It's good to make this an informal process, over drinks and snacks, if you can.
COMB	COMB is an excellent way to start any meeting: *Context* — Why you called the meeting *Objectives* — What you want the meeting to achieve *Map* — The agenda you propose to follow *Benefits* — What participants will get from contributing
Project context and objectives review	Look at the project context (Figure 4.2) and definition, and review key documents (Table 4.1)
Risk identification	Use a selection of the techniques from the next section of this chapter to identify risks.
Risk analysis	Explain the process you want to use and facilitate a discussion that will help the team to understand and evaluate the risks it has identified. This will include: • Likelihoods • Impacts • Overall prioritisation
Risk allocation	Whilst it is unlikely you will want to start planning responses to the risks in your workshop, you may want to allocate risk owners – particularly to the risks assessed as the highest priority. If you do so, consider seeking a commitment to each risk with specific actions or progress, to a specific deadline.
Next steps review	Finish your workshop with a summary of what the team has agreed, what actions each person has committed to, and the next steps for you and for the team. (The last thing you should do is thank your colleagues for their contributions.)

Some Tips and Tricks

Preparation is everything. A well prepared workshop can be fun and productive yet, with the same project and the same people, an unprepared workshop can be an unpleasant and unproductive waste of everybody's time. This may be the first time that some of your colleagues have experienced your leadership style. First impressions matter; don't blow it!

You may want to participate in the workshop discussions, or you may be unused to chairing a discussion and garnering contributions. If this is the case, consider bringing an external facilitator into the workshop. This need not be an expensive consultant; a suitably experienced colleague will be equally effective.

At various stages, issues and ideas may emerge in the meeting that are not strictly relevant to your agenda. Don't lose them. Keep a "car park" flipchart sheet available to note these down and assign the topic to somebody present to follow up after the meeting.

Document all ideas that emerge, all agreements reached and all commitments made. Do so using flipcharts or white boards, so that everyone can see that their idea has been captured; share a common statement of what is agreed. At the end of the meeting take photos of all boards and flipcharts as a back-up.

Within the next 24 hours, follow up the workshop with a written note of the commitments each person made and the next steps. If you did the "next steps" review at the end, this should be straightforward. Another "thank you" will also go down well.

SPOTTING RISKS

Now we have reached the point where we can look for risks: both threats and opportunities. There are six basic approaches: we will look at them in turn, illustrating each with some useful tools and techniques.

1. Personal Experience

Harnessing the experiences of the people in your team or organisation is a great starting place. Most of us are familiar with brainstorming, which is a staple of risk workshops. Table 4.4 sets out and describes six additional techniques.

Table 4.4: Risk Identification Using Personal Experience	
Brainstorming	Ask all participants to suggest ideas. Write everything down and resist the urge to analyse until you are finished. Build on ideas and ensure everybody can contribute. The rules of brainstorming include: • Everyone contributes • Encourage wild ideas • All ideas are valid – and recorded • Combine ideas The process is important. Think about how you will facilitate the process to ensure the quieter, less confident team members do not get shouted down by louder, more assertive colleagues. If you have too many people, how will you ensure you capture all of the ideas?
Brainwriting	Often more productive than brainstorming, particularly with a large group, each participant writes their ideas on separate cards (one per idea). In second and subsequent rounds, participants swap cards and modify each other's ideas or use them to stimulate a new idea, so that each card contains a trail of ideas and developments. Brainwriting can be useful when it is hard to make brainstorming work well.
Interviews	Interviews with colleagues and people with relevant experience can garner a lot of ideas and information. As always, prepare well and know what key questions you want to ask before starting the interview. This should free you up to listen hard, take notes and respond with follow-up questions.
Expert consultations	Sometimes, it is worth paying for advice from outside experts. This is usually a last resort in cases where there is little or no familiarity with what you are trying achieve.
Questionnaires	Questionnaires are a structured way to gather information from a lot of people that is less resource-intensive than interviews. Look at the many options the internet offers for free online questionnaires.
Mr/Ms Pessimistic	Do you know someone who always seems to see the downside of any new idea? You probably do. So sit them down, describe your project and, when they say, "I wouldn't do that if I were you...", ask them for 20 things they can anticipate going wrong. Some people's brains just seem wired to spot problems.
Pre-mortem	In his book, *The Power of Intuition*, Gary Klein describes a powerful process that asks participants to: 1. Relax 2. Imagine a fiasco 3. Generate reasons for that failure 4. Consolidate their lists

2. Horizon Scanning

Horizon scanning refers to techniques that try to look into the future to spot threats or opportunities. The master process for this is called scenario planning (which will be covered in Chapter 9). Three tools will help you with this.

SWOT analysis – Starting in the present, compile an analysis of your organisation's and team's strengths and weaknesses in the context of your project. Then review your findings, looking at how it offers opportunities or poses threats to the project.

Figure 4.3: SWOT Analysis

Strengths	Weaknesses
Opportunities	Threats

SPECTRES – There are a wide range of acronyms that act as prompt lists for sources of external threat and opportunity. Here is mine:

Table 4.5: SPECTRES	
Social	Social pressures and changes in society are especially an issue in the public and voluntary sectors, or in consumer-focused industries.
Political	Don't forget that politics is not just national, but local. In fact, in any office with two or more people, there's politics!
Economic	Externally, economic conditions may affect your project, but this should remind you of all of the financial pressures your project is under.
Competitive	If you work in a competitive environment, then this should remind you of your partners, competitors, customers, suppliers and their goodwill.
Technological	Luckily, technology never goes wrong. If only! Changes in technology also create threats and opportunities.
Regulatory	Understanding the legal and regulatory environment in which you work will help you identify risks; these conditions may change over a long project.
Environmental	Everyone is aware of environmental issues. But think local and immediate, too. Is your building conducive to effective project work?
Security	Threats to security abound, from terror, through vandalism, to theft. Consider each of these in turn.

Delphi Technique – The Delphi method is a structured way to pool the opinions of many experts to reach a group solution. It was developed in

1969 by the Rand Corporation to facilitate technological forecasting. It has the benefit of overcoming the bias that comes from some voices being more dominant than others – by virtue either of personality or eminence.

The primary uses of the Delphi method are in forecasting and decision making. The Delphi method tends to produce robust predictions based on experience, by eliminating the wilder contributions. However, when the past is a poor guide to the future and there is a possibility of massive and discontinuous change, the Delphi method is not suitable. This makes it inappropriate for leading edge projects. Here is a process for using the Delphi method for identifying and evaluating risks.

1. Select your panel of "experts" who will work on the problem.
2. Develop your initial set of questions, and send them to all participants. Ensure that as well as asking them for their ideas, you also elicit the reasoning behind their answers.
3. Analyse and tabulate the results, including the reasons, anonymously. Based on these results, prepare a second set of questions.
4. Return the analysis and reasons, along with the new questions, to all participants.
5. Continue looping back to step 3 until little or no change occurs. Then prepare your report and assess as required.

The Delphi technique eliminates need for group meetings and alleviates some of the bias they can create by removing the impact of dominant individuals. It also allows participants to change their minds anonymously. However, it can take a lot of time to reach a consensus, during which some participants may drop out. And beware: it is not as scientific as it appears.

Take care that the form of your questions does not introduce bias, and neither does your choice and balance of "experts". Independence and diversity is the key to success.

3. Accessing Data

If you search, you may be able to access a host of data to prompt your search for risks. We have already seen an example of a Risk Breakdown Structure in Figure 2.5. Other useful sources are:

- industry benchmarks and reports; often compiled by trade bodies, membership organisations and professional services firms that specialise in the sector
- tables and checklists of risks, like the one in Appendix A; a good industry example is Tom Kendrick's PERIL database
- a risk categorisation, such as the one in Table 4.6 below.

Table 4.6: Risk Categories

Marketplace risks	Technical risks	People risks	Process risks	Property risks	Financial risks
Competitors Customers Suppliers Contractors Consultants Partners Joint ventures Reputation / Goodwill Relationships	Security Requirements Interfaces Software Hardware Safety Reliability Maintenance	Capacity Capability Contractual terms Personal Key person Liability Applied to: Clients Staff Public Volunteers	Management Project Management Operational Governance Communications Resilience / continuity Health & Safety Technology Infrastructure Product failure	Security Premises Equipment Vehicles Financial assets Materials / stock Data	Interest rates Exchange rates Cash availability Liquidity Credit Debtors Profit

4. Organisational Memory

We will look in detail at the risk culture of organisations in Chapter 13 and how to facilitate a process of learning lessons from your project. If your predecessors have done this well and your organisation has retained the information in an accessible manner, then reports from previous projects can be a huge asset. Don't forget, too, that a vast store of organisational memory resides in a company's staff. Does your organisation have an archivist, or back issues of internal magazines, or a formal knowledge management system? Where they exist, refer to all of these.

5. Root Cause Analysis

There are a number of techniques that will allow you to get at the cause of a problem like "we ran out of money" or "the project over-ran" and so identify the underlying risk. Let's survey three of them.

Fishbone Method – Also known as the Ishikawa method, after its founder, the Fishbone method is ideal for getting to causes. To follow this method, draw a Fishbone diagram, putting the problem at the head of the fish.

Figure 4.4: Fishbone Diagram

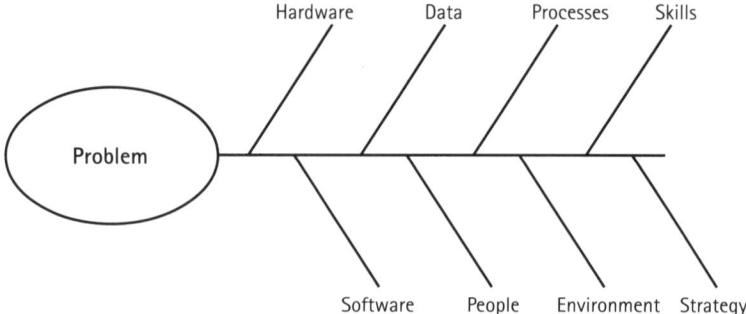

Then identify all of the possible causes and place each onto a "rib". In the example illustrated, there are eight typical sources of a problem. We might then break each one down further, identifying different reasons why the hardware, data, processes or skills might be causing the problem.

Figure 4.5: Fishbone Diagram, stage 2

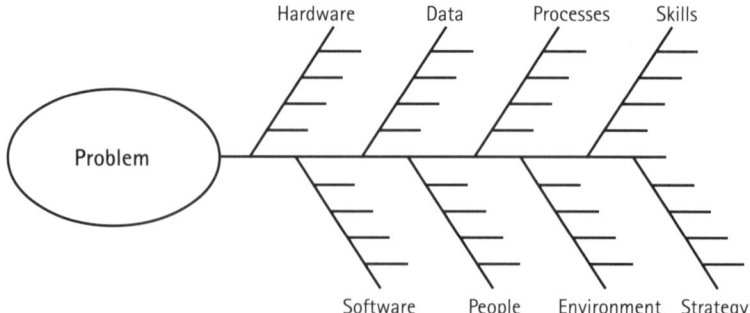

With "skills", for example, the cause could be:
- Lack of training
- Inappropriate training
- Poor workplace support for developing skills
- Poor motivation to use the skills

Some methodologies offer you a predetermined set of "causes". In the manufacturing sector, the 5M approach uses machinery, manpower, materials, methods and money. The McKinsey 7S model offers strategy, systems, staff, skills, style, shared values and structure. PESTLE analysis focuses on political, economic, social, technology, legal and environmental factors. And don't forget SPECTRES, the risk categories in Table 4.6, or the Risk Breakdown Structure in Figure 2.5.

Five Whys – If the Fishbone method identifies too many causes, then look for the one cause that is at the very root of the problem. We can find this by asking why? again and again. The Five Whys approach can help you to get to the root of the problem quickly. The method became popular in the 1970s as part of the Toyota Production System. You can take any problem and ask why it has happened. Often, the answer to the first why? will prompt another question and the answer to the second why? will prompt another, and so on. Repeat this until the root cause of the problem becomes apparent.

You do not necessarily have to ask the question five times. Sometimes, you can get to the root of the problem with fewer steps; sometimes you need more.

5W2H – These seven questions about a potential adverse outcome will give you the basis for systematic investigation:

What? Why? When? Where? Who? How often? How much/how many?

6. Project Analysis

The final approach to risk identification involves analysing your project plan in detail. In Chapter 2, we introduced the Work Breakdown Structure (WBS). You can use your WBS as the basis for identifying risks by examining each task at the lowest level and spotting the risks associated with it. The diagram in Figure 4.6 is formally known as a Process Decision Programme Chart, and illustrates the approach.

Figure 4.6: Process Decision Programme Chart

```
                    Village Hall
                  Opening Ceremony
         ┌────────────┼────────────┐
     1 Logistics   2 Catering    3 Guests
     1.1 Ribbon ceremony   2.1 Food preparation   3.1 Guest list
     1.2 Memoral plaque    2.2 Drink supply       3.2 Inviting guests
     1.3 Parking           2.3 Service            3.3 Greeting and assisting
                                                     3.3.1 Welcoming
                                                     3.3.2 Special needs
                                                     3.3.3 Guest of honour

      Cancellation        Cancellation              Late
      without             at last                   arrival
      notice              minute
      /    \              /    \            /      |      \
   Idea   Idea         Idea   Idea        Idea   Idea   Idea
```

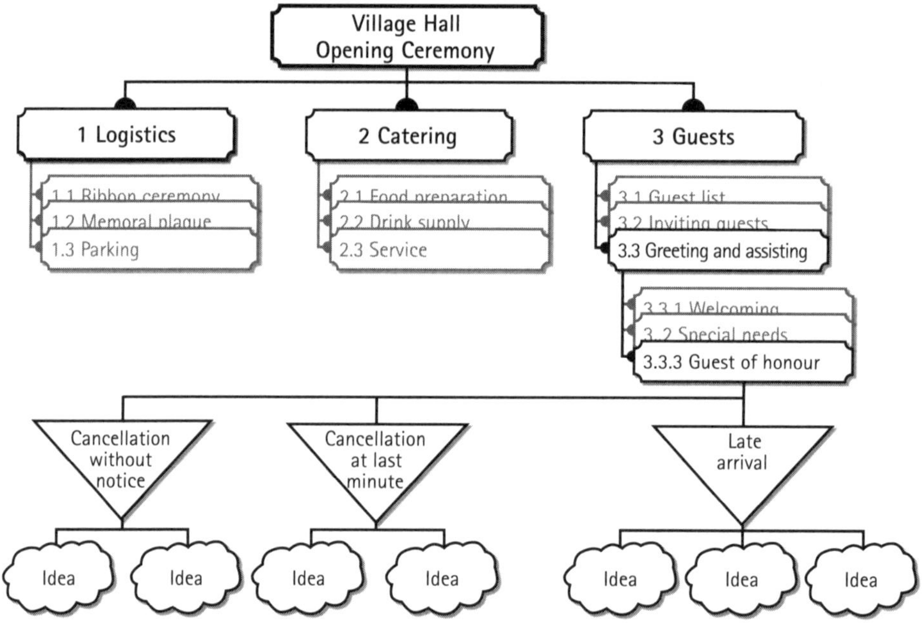

At the bottom of the chart, in the bubbles, you can document the ideas that address the risks.

DONALD RUMSFELD ON RISK

❝ *There are known knowns. These are things we know that we know. There are known unknowns. That is to say, there are things that we now know we don't know. But there are also unknown unknowns. These are things we do not know we don't know.*"

Donald Rumsfeld, US Secretary of Defense, 2001–2006

So far, we have been focusing on the "known unknowns". By definition, we can't get very far with the "unknown unknowns"; these are the stuff of scientific research, serendipity and unexplained calamity.

There is one area that too few people talk about, however: "unknown knowns". These are things that are known within your organisation – maybe even within your project – which nobody talks about. The subject may be too raw or, conversely, it maybe something taken for granted... which may not be true. In your quest to spot risks, take on the challenge to find some unknown knowns, and challenge them.

RISK REGISTER: THE PROJECT RISK MANAGER'S MULTITOOL

Perhaps the single most important risk management tool is a risk register (sometimes called a risk log). It has two principal purposes, both of which are equally important.

Audit Trail – Most of us now work in environments where accountability and good governance are essential. Your risk register provides a record of your risk process from identification, to analysis, planning, action and review. It shows the extent to which your actions have been diligent, prudent and reasonable.

Management Tool – Even if you didn't need an audit trail, your risk register will be the basis of day-to-day risk management actions, and of monitoring and controlling the risk aspects of your project.

One Step at a Time

Your risk register will support each step in our risk process, so we will build up a description of its functionality over the coming chapters. In this chapter, we will begin with some of the basic functions related to the identification stage.

Table 4.7 shows the beginning of a risk register, where the fields cover the identification components of the register. This is a simple version of a risk register. Yours may be more complex, or indeed even simpler, depending on the needs of your project. Below the table is a description of how to use each of its columns.

Table 4.7: Risk Register – Part 1				
Unique ID	Risk originator	Short description of risk	Full description of risk	...

Unique risk ID – As your risk register is likely to be part of a formal audit trail it is wise to allocate each risk a unique reference number. A simple 001–nnn sequence is perfectly adequate, but you could also use references derived either from a Risk Breakdown Structure or from your Work Breakdown Structure if you have used a process decision programme chart. The important thing is that if you remove a risk from your register for any reason, no new risk ever gets allocated a previously used number.

Risk originator – This is the person who originally identified the risk. This enables you to go back to him/her for clarification later. It is also possible to record an event, e.g. "Risk Workshop, 3 Jun 2012", in this field.

Short description of risk – This is a useful descriptor of the risk that you can use day-to-day to refer to the risk. It allows anyone to understand what the threat or opportunity is, and to distinguish it from other risks.

Full description of risk – You may well not refer to a full description of the risk at all on a smaller and more informal project. However, formally it is worth having a full description of the risk, even if you do not use it day-to-day.

Identify Risks

A formal description of a risk has four components, although some may not be relevant to all risks. These components arise from the cause and effect nature of risk and are shown in Table 4.8.

Table 4.8: Formal Description of a Risk			
A pre-existing condition ...	... can be triggered by a particular circumstance ...	... to create a causal event ...	... that leads to a change in the project outcome
Root cause	*Trigger*	*Risk*	*Consequence*

Not all risk events have a discernable trigger, but you can scan for it as part of your monitoring process. An example might be the effect of a heavy snow storm on a house-building project. The root cause would be a schedule that has major construction works happening at the end of the winter period, in early March. The trigger would be the appearance of a heavy depression moving towards the site. The risk is the snow storm itself, and the consequence is a 7–14 week delay to the programme.

If you are able to spot the triggering event early enough, whilst you cannot stop the snow storm, you could prevent the pouring of concrete foundations the day before, when to do so risks the concrete failing to set fully to its required strength. The consequence of this would be a need to dig up the weak concrete and re-lay it at substantial added cost and delay.

Figure 4.7: The Formal Structure of a Risk

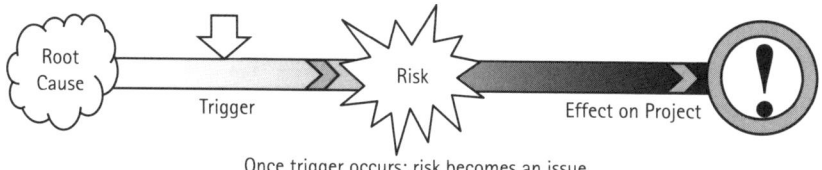

Once trigger occurs; risk becomes an issue

Suitable Software

The tool you use to create and maintain your risk register is a matter of preference and practicality. Many organisations have their own proforma or template; if you don't, it is easy to create one. Of course the simplest is a table in your notebook or project file – for the smallest of projects, this is perfectly adequate. However, if you are subject to audit, it would be wise to "back it up" by photocopying it each week and storing the copy in a separate archive.

As for computer software solutions, you could use a word-processor, spreadsheet or a database. For all but the largest projects, a spreadsheet is the best method; you can download a sample spreadsheet risk register from *www.riskhappens.co.uk*.

The advantages of a spreadsheet over a table is convenience. With a spreadsheet, you can easily:

- Hide columns or rows
- Insert columns or rows
- Perform calculations
- Filter for specific criteria
- Sort according to any number of fields
- Export to a range of applications
- Perform basic database functions
- Create charts and tables for reporting
- Share the whole – or portions – of the register
- Prepare reports from your risk register

A database solution – whether one you build yourself or a proprietary one – can give you still more functionality. However, it is rare that on any but the largest project you will need this extra functionality. It will be hard to justify the additional overhead of installation and configuration costs, purchase cost or development time, and learning requirement. However, on a complex and large project, this could be a valuable investment.

CHAPTER 5
ANALYSE RISKS

ONCE YOU HAVE IDENTIFIED the project risks, your next step is to analyse those risks to gain a more thorough understanding. If you have been disciplined enough to define each risk formally, as in Table 4.8, you have already made a good start. Four further analytical approaches remain:
1. Categorising your risks
2. Evaluating them qualitatively
3. Evaluating them quantitatively
4. Prioritising your risks for action

The more work you do at this stage, the better prepared you will be to design an effective plan and manage the risk. As always, there is a law of diminishing return, so use your judgement to avoid paralysis through over-analysis.

This chapter explores all four analytical approaches. We will, however, focus most closely on qualitative analysis. There is a spectrum that runs from pure qualitative analysis, based entirely on subjective and unmeasurable characteristics, through to purely quantitative analysis, built from verifiable data in a numerical format. In between is what we could describe as pseudo-quantitative analysis. This is qualitative analysis dressed up as quantitative analysis, using numbers and mathematics that seem scientific but are nothing more than plausible arguments that source numbers back to estimates and subjective judgements. A lot of risk analysis is of this type.

We shall be literal and consider these as qualitative, seeing through the light clothing of apparent mathematical rigour. Truly quantitative analysis is most often used to combine the effects of multiple risks in projects that are sufficiently large to justify the considerable effort that it takes to do this well.

CATEGORISE YOUR RISKS

There are a lot of different ways to categorise risks. So, before you begin, always ask yourself this question: *Once I have classified my risks into categories, how will I use that classification to assist me in managing, controlling, reducing or eliminating them?*

This question is important for two reasons:

- If you don't have a good answer, then it is very likely that the work of categorising your risks will be wasted effort.
- If you do have a good answer, it will help you to determine which categories will best serve your project.

There are two bases for categorising your risks.

By Cause

The SPECTRES framework (Table 4.5) gives you a great starting place for allocating categories. These are, of course, all "external" causes of risk. You may also want to note "internal" causes such as people, process and technology. You could use Table 4.6 to further breakdown your internal risk categories. You may find that a simple classification of your risks as either internal or external is all you need.

By Outcome

It is also possible to classify risks according to how or where the disruption or opportunity will strike your project. This is the basis of the Risk Breakdown Structure in Figure 2.5, and its top level structure on time (or schedule), cost (or budget), scope and quality may be a helpful classification. You may alternatively use your Work Breakdown Structure to identify what work-streams or product areas the risks threaten.

Another helpful distinction to make when you are thinking about outcomes is whether the potential disruption is "fixed" or "variable". A "fixed" risk is one where if the risk manifests, the disruption is a clearly defined amount of time, cost, functionality, reputational damage, etc. On the other hand, "variable" risks give rise to an uncertain level of disruption, dependent upon circumstances. For example, we may be constructing an extension to a building. The risk of bad weather causing delays and cost over-runs is a variable risk, because the level of disruption depends on the severity of the weather and how long the adverse conditions last. The failure of a supplier to be able to source a particular component or materials is a fixed risk if you have an alternative supplier who has quoted a firm alternative delivery date and price.

QUALITATIVE ANALYSIS

> ❝Fear of harm ought to be proportional not merely to the gravity of the harm, but also to the probability of the event.❞

So wrote Antoine Arnauld and Pierre Nicole in 1662. Ever since then, it has been understood that risk can be analysed in terms of its impact and its likelihood. Indeed, this flows from our definition of risk: uncertainty that can affect outcomes. Likelihood measures the uncertainty, and impact measures the effect on outcomes.

We will start by considering likelihood, then impact, then two other qualitative characteristics – triggers and proximity – and then end this section on qualitative analysis by looking at ways to represent your risks graphically.

The Trouble with Likelihood

Estimating likelihoods for project risks is an extremely problematic task. Human beings are extremely poor at estimating the likelihood of uncertain events. This is because we are equipped with a set of biases that confuse the issue and rapidly lead us astray. Here are three of the commonest examples (you will find a lot more about the psychological factors of risk estimation in Chapter 12).

Control Bias

We tend to think bad things are less likely to occur when we are in control – which makes sense. The problems arise when we are not in control, but somebody else is. Our own "passenger" status then leads us to over-estimate the risk, even when the person who is in control is very capable. Most people feel safer when they are driving than when somebody else is – regardless of the other person's safety record. Many people feel safer driving than on public transport, despite the overwhelming weight of statistics showing travelling on public transport is safer.

Recency

"But what", some people will say, "about the pilot who was drinking in the cockpit, or the bus driver who was using a mobile phone?" These are examples of how recent newsworthy events can take over our consciousness and lead us to over-estimate the probability of a recurrence. Strangely, the millions of bus journeys in which no incident occurs are never reported, and neither is each safe airplane landing. Perhaps our attitudes would change if every road traffic accident were on the news.

Dread

The worse the outcome, the higher we will rate it on the impact scale. We also seem to unconsciously adjust our estimation of likelihood according to the perceived seriousness of the impact. In our imaginations, higher impact events seem more likely to occur. In the real world, most uncertain events cluster around a diagonal line on our familiar "Impact versus Likelihood" graph: highly likely events tend to be low impact, whilst high impact events tend to be rare. Yet we often distort our estimates to reflect our fears.

Solving the Probability Problem
Unless you are an expert in something, you will never have sufficient data and analytical tools to estimate probabilities accurately. So the first solution is simple: don't try!

Perceived Frequency Estimates
If you try to estimate likelihood with accuracy, you risk falling into another trap: The "precision trap". This is where you mistake precision for accuracy; the more precise your estimate, the more convincing it seems. To avoid the precision trap, the safest route is to stick to low-precision estimates. Avoid the temptation to use too many categories on the likelihood scale of your risk assessment. Absolutely reject the use of probability-based likelihood estimates unless you have real data on which to base your probabilities and you also have a good understanding of statistics and probability theory.

My favourite scale for likelihood is this:
- *High*: The sort of things that seem to happen a lot – most of us have experienced them and we all know people who have.
- *Medium*: The sort of things that seem to happen from time to time – a few of us have experienced them and most of us know someone who has.
- *Low*: The sort of things that do happen from time to time – though few of us know someone who has actually experienced them.

You might implement five levels if you feel you need a greater level of discrimination, but more is definitely being over precise. You can improve the judgement you make on this sort of scale by polling several people and looking at the range and average of their answers before settling on an estimate.

If all this still sounds imprecise, then it is supposed to. It is best if project managers don't believe their risk estimates – but rather that you act on best evidence and good judgement. A more rigorous way to harness different people's opinions is to apply the Delphi Technique described in Chapter 4, under Horizon Scanning.

Historical Data

Who are the people that are best at estimating the likelihood of risks? If you thought "bookmakers" then you are wrong. All they do is accurately collate the estimates of the people who make bets and calculate odds that are designed to make them a profit regardless of the outcome. They are not at all interested in the actual likelihoods of different outcomes of the race, match or other event.

The answer is "actuaries" – the people who calculate the risks involved in insurance policies. The reason they can be accurate is that they have good historical data, averaged over many policy holders,. What makes this technique tricky for you, as a project manager, is that projects tend to be one-off endeavours: there is little or no historical data, and the number of instances of similar projects is often limited – even if you can satisfy yourself that there is enough similarity to make the comparison a fair one.

Descriptive Labels

A common approach is to use descriptive labels for bands of likelihood. Table 5.1 gives some typical examples.

Table 5.1: Typical Descriptors for Likelihood

Very Low	Low	Medium	High	Very High
Rare occurrence	Occasional occurrence	Intermittent occurrence	Frequent occurrence	Routine occurrence
Very unlikely	Possible	Could well happen	Quite likely	Virtually certain
Highly unlikely	Unlikely	Evens	Likely	Highly probable
Improbable	Remote	Occasional	Probable	Frequent

These approaches seem appealing. The words probably conjure up reasonably robust categories in your mind. The problem is that the categories that you imagine are almost certainly different from the categories I see in my mind! In a paper presented to the Project Management Institute Global Congress in 2005, Dr David Hillson describes a survey of over 500 people interested in risk management – the very people who ought to think most clearly in this area. He found a large spread of interpretations of phrases like these.

Probability Estimates

If you must use probability estimates, do so with care. The categories that organisations often use are, frankly, absurd. Look at Table 5.2 and then discard it immediately.

Table 5.2: Typical Probability Ranges for Likelihood					
Very Low	Low	Medium	High	Very High
Below 10%	10–50%	51–75%	76–90%	Over 90%
Please note: the content of this table is nonsense. It is taken from the risk management guidance principles of a very large UK-based organisation; but under this classification, a 5% likelihood would be seen as the lowest risk level and the risk would probably be ignored. Yet this is a one in 20 chance. If this were applied to a motor vehicle accident, or every time we crossed a road, it would no longer seem a small risk.				

It is the nature of rare events that they tend to follow what mathematicians describe as a "power law". This means that big, high-threat events are very rare, but small, minor inconveniences are very common. A good set of probability categories should reflect the exponential nature of a power law. Table 5.3 gives some suggested approaches, but please note that the apparent numerical rigour it appears to offer hides the fact that where you estimate your risk to lie will still usually be little more than a matter of personal judgement – with all the subjective biases that this implies.

Table 5.3: Suggested Probability Ranges for Likelihood

Very Low	Low	Medium	High	Very High
Below 5%	5–10%	11–25%	26–50%	Over 50%
Below 1%	1–3%	4–10%	11–33%	Over 33%
Once in 100 years	Once in 30 years	Once in 10 years	Once in 3 years	Once a year

Measuring Impact

Impact is far easier to estimate reliably, and we will examine a number of different ways that you could do this. First, let's review why *impact* is a better word than the frequently used alterative, *severity*. Severity seems to imply a numerical measure of impact; while impact also suggests a sense of what will happen:

Severity: how good or bad something is

Impact: the ways in which something is good or bad

Impact therefore invites us to consider the consequences of a risk, as well as how good or bad they may be. There are numerous bases for categorising impact. In determining what scale to use, follow this two step process:

1. Determine what basis is most appropriate to your project. You may need several scales on different bases. The examples we will look at are a general scale, schedule, financial, quality, scope, reputational, health and safety, security and environmental.
2. For each basis that is relevant, work with colleagues to determine a scale that best suits your environment. The tables below set out example scales that you can either use or adapt to your own needs.

Table 5.4: Suggested General Scales for Impact

Very Low	Low	Medium	High	Very High
Minor	Moderate	Significant	Substantial	Big
Corrective action needed	Adjustments to plan needed	Revised strategy needed	One or more objectives threatened	Project goal would not be achieved
				more >>>

Analyse Risks 67

Little or no impact	Requires Team Leader attention	Requires Project Manager attention	Requires Project Sponsor attention	Requires Attention from organisational leadership team

Note that you may want to define a mega impact where the impact goes beyond your project and harms the organisation in some greater way.

Table 5.5: Suggested Scales for Schedule Impact

Very Low	Low	Medium	High	Very High
Insignificant impact	Less than 3%	3–10%	11–33%	More than 33%
Less than 5%	5–10%	11–25%	26–50%	More than 50%
No delay	Minor delays to work stream can be made up	Project contingency threatened	Minor project delay	Significant project delay

Table 5.6: Suggested Scales for Financial Impact

Very Low	Low	Medium	High	Very High
Insignificant impact	Less than 10%	11–33%	34–100%	More than 100%
Less than 5%	5–10%	11–25%	26–50%	More than 50%
No cost incurred	Small costs contained within budget contingency	Project over-budget	Project return diminished; business case threatened	No return on investment; project deemed a failure
Less than £1,000	£1,000–£5,000	£5,000 + £10,000	£10,000 + £50,000	More than £50,000
Hundreds of pounds	Thousands of pounds	Tens of thousands of pounds	Hundreds of thousands of pounds	Millions of pounds

You can shift the last of two of these scales up or down, depending on the size of your organisation. A government or multinational conglomerate might scale up to billions and beyond.

Table 5.7: Suggested Scales for Quality Impact

Very Low	Low	Medium	High	Very High
Quality drop only detectable by expert analysis	Minor quality drop	Significant quality drop	Unacceptable quality	Failure to function
Easy to fix	Fix requires investigation	Difficult to fix	Complex and costly to fix	Impossible to fix
Team Leader can approve	Project manager can approve	Design authority can approve	Project sponsor / project board would need to approve	Unacceptable

Table 5.8: Suggested Scales for Scope Impact

Very Low	Low	Medium	High	Very High
Trivial	Small scope changes needed	Significant scope changes needed	Major scope changes needed	Fundamental change to project
Team Leader can approve	Project manager can approve	Design Authority can approve	Project sponsor / project board would need to approve	Project sponsor / project board would need to re-evaluate project

Table 5.9: Suggested Scales for Reputational Impact

Very Low	Low	Medium	High	Very High
None	Low level local or trade press publicity	Prominent local or trade press publicity	National publicity	National headlines
Operational Issue	Head of PR / communications team matter	Divisional director matter	Senior director matter	Chair, CEO, ministerial matter
Attracts comment among stakeholders	Loss of confidence among stakeholders	Press criticisms	Widespread criticism	Long term loss of confidence
One of those things	Project Manager embarrassed	Project Manager severely embarrassed	Project Sponsor embarrassed	CEO or minister embarrassed
For mega level impacts, senior level resignations may be expected.				

Table 5.10: Suggested Scales for Health, Safety or Security Impact

Very Low	Low	Medium	High	Very High
No injuries	Minor injuries	Major injuries	A fatality	Multiple fatalities
Minor breach of regulations	Enforcement notice	Prosecution	Short-term stoppage or closure	Long-term stoppage or closure
For mega level impacts or large scale fatalities, corporate manslaughter charges and closure of the business are potential outcomes.				

Table 5.11: Suggested Scales for Environmental Impact

Very Low	Low	Medium	High	Very High
None	Local damage	Widespread damage	Regional damage	National damage
No damage	Minor damage will resolve quickly	Major damage will require active clean-up	Long-lasting damage	Permanent damage

Likelihood-Impact Chart

One of the clearest and most basic analyses of risk is to place each potential risk in a band for its impact and its likelihood, which gives you a diagram that looks like Figure 5.1.

Figure 5.1: Likelihood versus Impact Chart

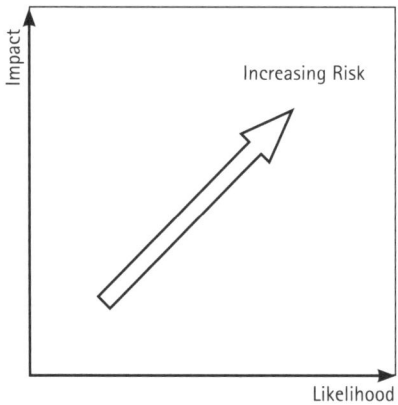

Times Tables

As human beings, we like to simplify things as much as we can, and in this case, it is common practice to reduce a risk to a single measure, rather than the two measures of likelihood and impact. Observing the chart in Figure 5.1, it should be evident that risks that are nearer the top right corner are a greater concern than those at the bottom left.

This leads to the common practice of producing a single measure of "how big the risk is" by looking at how far the risk lies along the line of increasing risk. We can assign this a numerical measure, simply by assigning a numerical score to each of the likelihood and impact categories. The commonest practice is illustrated in Table 5.12.

Table 5.12: Frequently Used Numerical Scale for Likelihoods and Impacts				
Very Low	Low	Medium	High	Very High
1	2	3	4	5

70 RISK HAPPENS!

Combining the likelihood and impact scores is then simply a matter of choosing a mathematical way of combining two numbers. Whilst adding will work, the chart in Figure 5.2 reminds us of a multiplication table, of the type we learned at school.

Figure 5.2: Likelihood versus Impact Chart, with scoring

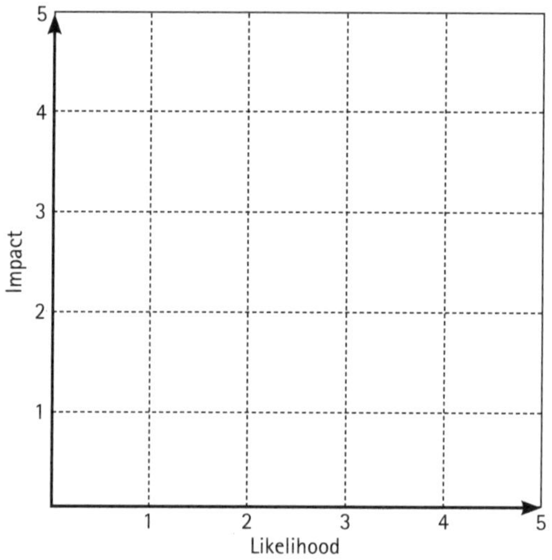

[Chart showing a 5x5 grid with Impact on the y-axis (1 to 5) and Likelihood on the x-axis (1 to 5)]

The reason that this is superior to simple addition is easily seen by comparing two extremes: a bad risk with scores of 5 and 5, with a minor risk with scores of 1 and 1. If we were to use addition, the measures of risk would be 10 and 2 respectively, so the worst possible risk would seem only 5 times as bad as the least possible risk. If we multiply, the respective scores are 1 and 25. The ratio here is more plausible...

The Problems with Scoring

... but not entirely convincing. After all, a risk that is highly likely to occur and could end the project, create national headlines and cost hundreds of thousands of pounds is here rated as only 25 times as bad as an extremely unlikely event that will, at worst, cause some minor inconvenience.

If you are going to use scores for anything more than simple prioritisation or ranking of risks, exponential scales are far more appropriate.

Table 5.13: Example of an Exponential Numerical Scale for Likelihoods and Impacts

Very Low	Low	Medium	High	Very High
1	2	4	8	16

Scoring is fine, as long as you only use it for two things:
- Initial prioritisation
- As a *support* for decision making, rather than as *the process for* decision making

Here are some of the failings of a scoring system.

Table 5.14: Failings of Risk Scoring Systems

1. The scores give only the appearance of precision and objectivity – they are often based on purely subjective assessments.
2. Single point estimates for the impact and probability of a risk are rarely reliable. Our best estimate of likelihood should be a range; in variable risks (see risk classification earlier in this chapter), the impact will also be best represented by a range.
3. If likelihood and impact are really ranges, then combining them through multiplication is mathematically flawed and represents, at best, a very crude approximation to the true outcome.
4. Users tend to steer away from the extremes of the scales, so that in a five point scale from 1–5 most risks will usually cluster around the middle. In real world data sets, the distribution you should expect is a peak near the minimum.
5. Some risks will be seriously underestimated in impact or likelihood, resulting from bias towards over-optimism or over-confidence in your team's abilities.
6. Getting a scale that fairly represents the relative weights of the different levels of probability or impact is an onerous analytical task. To do it properly would need a careful study for each new situation.
7. Risks are rarely independent of one another. None of this apparently logical structure in any way represents the inter-dependence that will exist between the risks you have identified. Figure 5.3 shows how you can start to understand the inter-relatedness of your risks using a dependency map.

If you count the number of arrows originating from each risk in Figure 5.3, you can get a simple indication of which risks are the more fundamental.

Figure 5.3: Risk Dependency Map

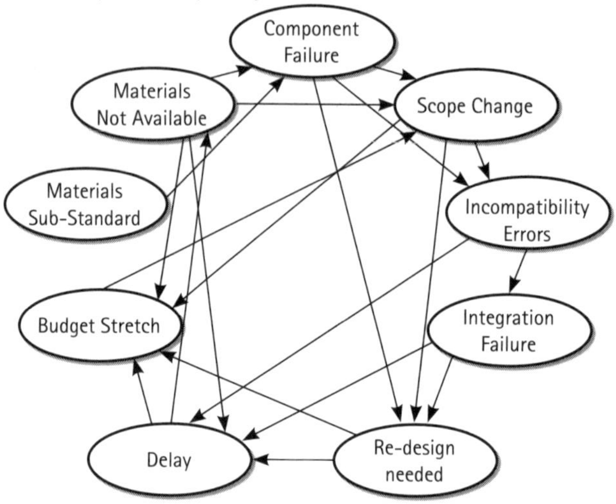

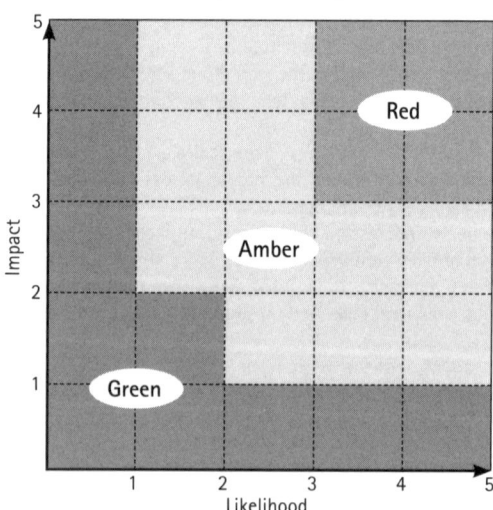

Colouring Your Risk Chart

In the light of all of these problems, a simpler solution is to colour the cells in Figure 5.2, to give a chart like the one in Figure 5.4.

Figure 5.4: Likelihood versus Impact Chart, with colour zones

Typically the colours red, amber and green are used, in reference to the colours of a traffic light. This gives each risk a "RAG status" or "Traffic

Light status". Users would then create a standard interpretation for each status, like the ones in Table 5.15 below. This also includes additional status colours that you may sometimes see, or may find useful.

Table 5.15: Traffic Light Status Definitions	
Red	*Severe threat* – Often Red designates risks that will not be tolerated, but equally, this zone may just mean that the risks require multiple strategies to manage them. These risks will certainly be notified to the project sponsor and the project board and be monitored by them.
Amber (or orange)	*Serious risks* – These demand to be addressed with a risk management plan. These will certainly receive the project manager's attention.
Green	*Minor risks* – These can be accepted without action and may not be formally reported on outside the project itself.
White	Sometimes white is used to designate risks that have been identified but have been assessed as not requiring further attention. These can safely be ignored. This will sit at the extreme bottom left of your chart.
Black	Sometimes black is used to designate the most serious threats to your project. They may have mega impacts and a reasonable likelihood of manifesting. However you define this zone (if you do), it will be at the very top right of your chart and any risks that fall into will receive the most careful planning, scrutiny and monitoring at all levels.
Blue	When reporting on risks, it is unwise to drop a risk that had a red or black status in your previous report from your new report. If the risk has been resolved and is no longer a threat, a blue status will signify this and alert the readers of your report that they will not see the risk reported on again. If you simply drop a risk from your report, you will invite unnecessary questions from alert readers.

Triggers

In Table 4.8, we saw that a pre-existing condition can be triggered by a particular circumstance to create a causal event that leads to a change in the project outcome. If you can identify the trigger in advance, you may be able to prevent the risk itself. Identify the early warning signals that you can monitor.

Proximity

When project managers talk about risk proximity, they are referring to the time between now and the first potential impact of the risk. We consider a threat to be greater as we approach it. This is why younger people frequently neglect their health, their health insurance and their pensions. It is not that they don't believe they will get unfit, unwell or old; it just seems a long way off. Measure proximity in days, weeks or months, or simply define near term, medium term and long term risks in terms of the typical time scale of your project.

It is also worth noting that our perception of risk is also affected by emotional proximity. We are biased to subjectively evaluate risks as greater the more closely we feel we would be touched by them. Geographical proximity is also a factor. Our response to threats close to home is greater than the equivalent threat to things far away.

Alternative Charts

A "Likelihood versus Impact" chart is by far the commonest way of illustrating risks. Figures 5.5 to 5.8 illustrate four further ways of representing risk graphically. One of the joys of project management are the opportunities offered to be creative in finding powerful ways to present your analysis.

QUANTITATIVE ANALYSIS

True quantitative analysis must be based on rigorous mathematical techniques and should ideally start with well-researched estimates. It is time-consuming and costly. Therefore, only the largest, most sensitive projects can justify a full quantitative analysis; a full description of the techniques involved is beyond the scope of this book. Here, you will get an introduction to three quantitative methods. The first two, the RMS method and "decision trees", are relatively straightforward to apply and are worth considering for a subset of the most serious risks on moderately large projects. The third, the Monte Carlo method, requires a lot of work and sophisticated software. There is a range of readily available software that can make the task simpler, but the simplification can negate a lot of the value of the method. This is, however, one the most important methods and one which any project risk manager will want to have at least a basic understanding of.

Figure 5.5: Time to impact versus Likelihood, with bubble size representing Impact

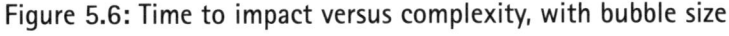

Figure 5.6: Time to impact versus complexity, with bubble size representing Impact

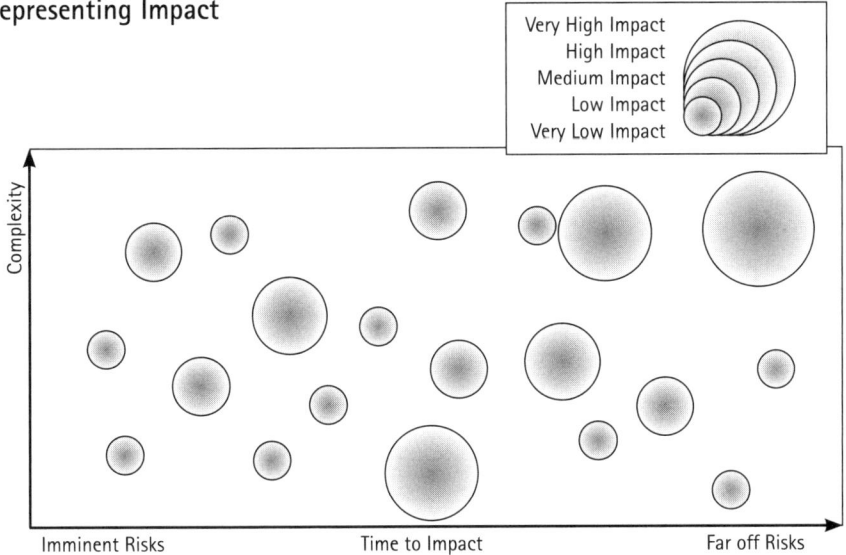

76　RISK HAPPENS!

Figure 5.7: Likelihoods of two independent events, with bubble size representing impact of combined outcome

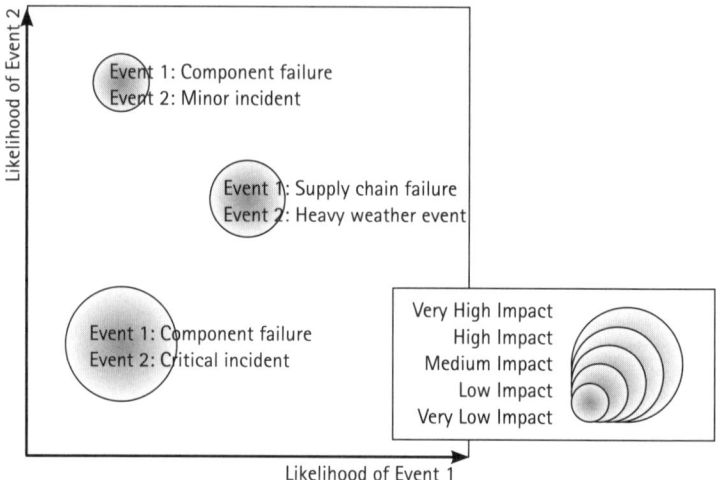

Figure 5.8: Budget impact versus Schedule impact, with bubble size representing Probability

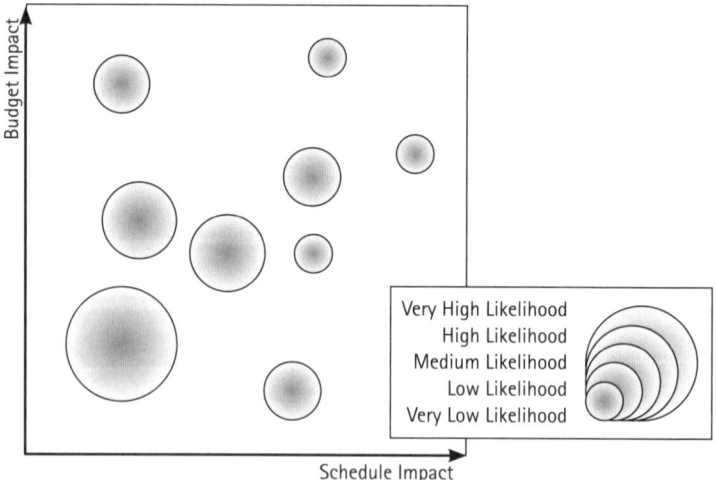

The RMS Method

Root Mean Squared (RMS) is a standard way of statistically combining estimates for multiple risks into a single risk value. The estimates that this method produces are useful and it is straightforward to set up the calculation on a spreadsheet. However, be warned that it remains reliant on the quality of individual estimates, which may be subjective.

Let's take an example: a project to renovate a dilapidated shed. In a brainstorming session, I identify around a dozen risks, but most are relatively minor and would involve only a little extra work and additional fixings. There are two significant risks to my base budget of £250, called my Risk Free Estimate:

- Risk 1: When I remove the glass to renovate the woodwork, I may shatter the panes and need to replace them at £45.
- Risk 2: Some of the structural timber may be rotten and need replacing.

From our discussion of risk classification earlier in the chapter, you will recognise Risk 1 as a fixed risk, and Risk 2 as variable, so we will treat each a little differently. First, I estimate the probability of breaking the glass and the full cost of replacing it. I can then calculate a Maximum Risk Value (MRV) and an Average Risk Value (ARV).

Table 5.16a: RMS Method – Risk 1			
Risk	Probability	Maximum Risk Value (MRV)	Average Risk Value (ARV)
1. Broken glass	33%	1.00 x £45 = £45	0.33 x £45 = £15

Risk 2 is a variable risk. I could need to replace all of the timbers or just one piece. Here, I have to make cost estimates for MRV and ARV. Conventionally, we allocate to ARV the cost we believe is equally likely to be exceeded or come under – the 50% confidence limit. For MRV, we can use the full potential cost, but unless we think this is a plausible scenario, we may take the 90% confidence limit. In this case, my shed is damp and I fear it may all be rotten.

Table 5.16b: RMS Method – Risk 2

Risk	Probability	Maximum Risk Value (MRV)	Average Risk Value (ARV)
2. Rotten timbers	N/A	1.00 x £70 = £70	0.50 x £70 = £35

Now we are ready to calculate the risk estimates. To do this I need to calculate the spreads, or differences, between my Average Risk Value (ARV) and Maximum Risk Value (MRV). I then square those spreads, and add them all up.

Table 5.16c: RMS Method – Calculation

Risk	Probability	Maximum Risk Value (MRV)	Average Risk Value (ARV)	Spread	Square of spread
1. Broken glass	33%	£45	£15	£30	900
2. Rotten timbers		£70	£35	£35	1,225
Totals		£115	£50		2,125

Our Risk Free Estimate, or base cost, was £250. Our ARE is calculated by adding the sum of the ARVs. To calculate our Maximum Likely Risk Estimate, we now add the square root of the sum of the squares of the spreads. In our example, the square root of 2,125 is £46. Of course, the Absolute Maximum Risk is the sum of all of the MRVs.

Table 5.16d: RMS Method – Results

Base Cost		£250
Average Risk Estimate	£250 + £50	£300
Maximum Likely Risk Estimate	£300 + £46	£346
Maximum Risk Estimate	£250 + £115	£365

A contingency of between £50 and £96 would be wise. The RMS method can equally be applied to schedule risks, too.

Decision Trees

Decision trees are a useful way to decide which of a number of alternative choices is most favourable. With too many options, it rapidly becomes unwieldy, but for simpler cases, it is a useful tool. Like the RMS method, this can be used for both schedule and budget risks, but again, it is more commonly applied to financial analysis.

Decision trees are best understood graphically, so Figure 5.9 gives an illustrative example. Here, the total cost of Remedial Option A is £24,000 and of Option B, £29,000. If all other considerations were equal – which of course they rarely are in the real world – then we would choose Option A.

Figure 5.9: Decision Tree Example

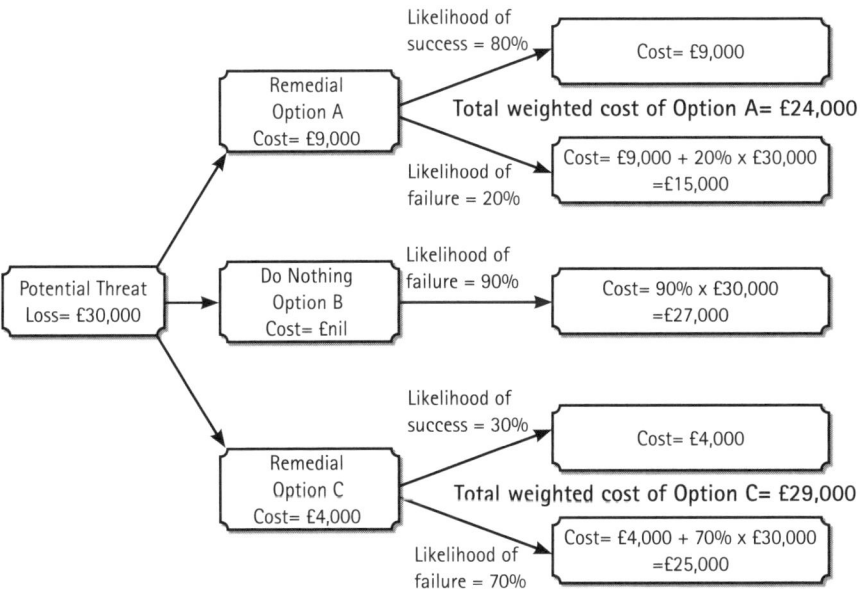

What would happen if there were a fourth Option D? This option is certain to avert the threat, but costs £35,000. Statistically, this is the least favoured option, but it does offer certainty. Many project managers would trade a little extra cost for this certainty. But how much? What if the cost of Option D were £40,000, or £50,000? This will depend upon the culture of your project and organisation, and certainly on good judgement.

The Monte Carlo Method

The Monte Carlo Method takes its names from the random chances at the gaming tables of Monte Carlo (and the name was used as a code name on the Manhattan Project – the secret US World War II plan to develop the atom bomb). Let's consider its application to schedule risk, where it is most often used, although it can also be used for budget risk. For each activity on the project, we need to estimate a range of probabilities for different possible durations. The set of durations and our estimates of their probability is called the "probability distribution" for the activity durations.

We saw this process in Chapter 2, when we examined the PERT method. The difference here is that rather than a probability distribution with three points, we need a whole distribution of estimates. The statistics of the PERT method are based on one possible spread of likelihoods, called the "beta function" by statisticians.

Figure 5.10: The Beta Function

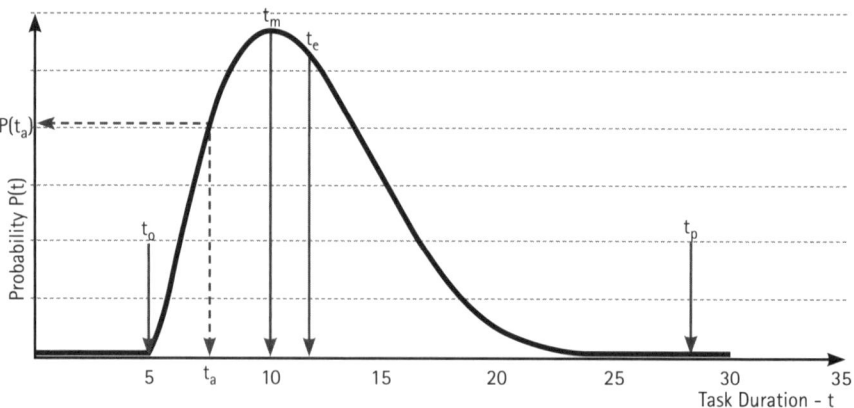

Other distributions each have their merits, but a discussion of this is not within the parameters of this book. In the real world, each task will have its own distribution of likelihoods of duration; some simple, some complex. Figure 5.11 illustrates a number of typical distributions of the probabilities of different activity durations. Each will apply to different types of activity.

Figure 5.11: Examples of Statistical Distributions

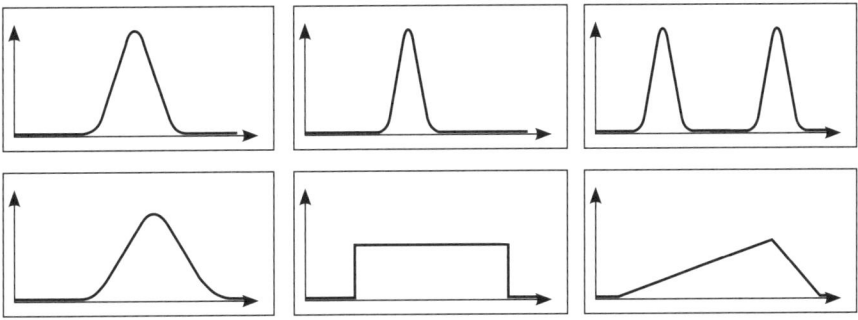

The Monte Carlo Method calculates how long the total project will take by adding up the durations of all of the activities, each with a duration randomly assigned. The probability of each task's duration is defined by the probability function in our curve. To simulate the random nature, the method repeats the calculation, with a different set of random durations many, many times. This gives a distribution of all of the possible total project durations.

The calculation is the easy part. Making the estimates of the probability distribution for each task is time-consuming and the quality of the estimates will entirely determine the validity of the resulting distribution. If all that you do is use the same distribution for each activity, you will simply reproduce that pattern for the whole project.

There is one other major flaw in the Monte Carlo Method, which renders its results far less reliable than you might think. It contains the implicit assumption that the probability distribution for each task is independent of all others. Yet we know that a delay in one activity can often make others more likely to be delayed too, and that one event can affect multiple tasks. As in all of risk management, the strides towards rigour have only got us so far, and there is no substitute for good judgement and appropriate scepticism and caution.

PRIORITISE YOUR RISKS

We have already seen two ways you can prioritise risks: RAG status, and the multiplication of likelihood and impact values. Flawed as both methods are, they offer a good guide to priorities. Let's examine another method.

Team Scoring of Risks

Give everybody in the team a copy of all of the risks that you have identified, and ask them to identify the top 10, allocating 10 points to that which they consider the greatest concern, 9 to the next, and so on down to 1. When everyone has done this, simply add up the scores for each risk.

Be sure to examine risks where one or two individuals have a very different perspective from the bulk of the group. Have they simply got it wrong, or have they instead spotted something important that everyone has overlooked? There is no substitute for discussion and exploration.

The "Sleep at Night Test"

When you have a ranked list of your risks, use your gut instinct to find a cut-off between the risks that will cause you to lose sleep and those that won't; this is a simple way to find your top tier of risks. If you do this with a group and everyone ranks the risk in order of where the cut-off is for them, you will get a distribution like the one in Figure 5.12. This will give you a more rounded basis to decide on your top tier of risks.

Figure 5.12: The "sleep at night test" Results

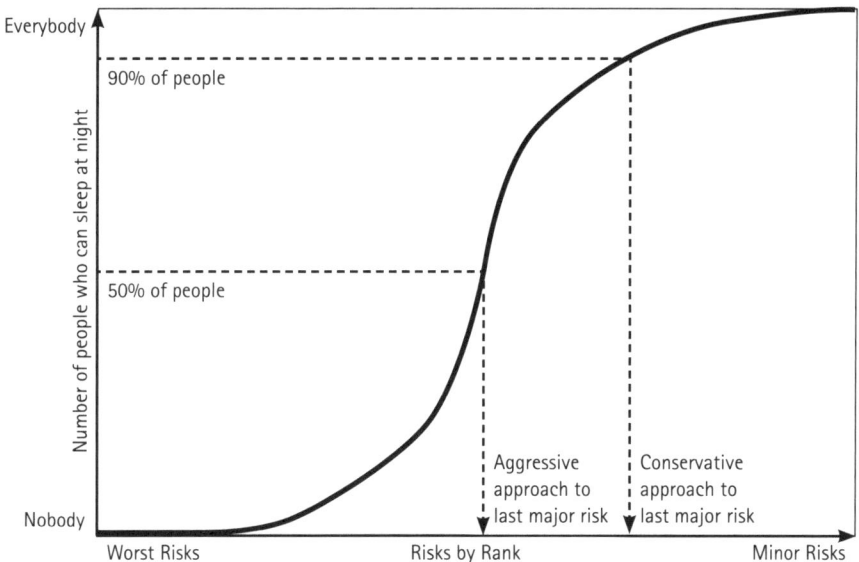

RISK REGISTER: RECORDING THE THREAT LEVEL

You are now ready to record your evaluation of your risks onto your risk register. Whilst there are many examples of more sophisticated registers, a basic approach is illustrated in Table 5.17.

...	Risk Category	Risk Evaluation				...
		Likelihood	Impact	Proximity	Score	

Table 5.17: Risk Register – Part 2

Risk Category – If you have chosen to categorise your risks, then here is where you would record the category against each risk. Only do this if you will use the information in your decision making or control processes.

Likelihood/Impact – These are often recorded with numerical scales, as described above, for example 1–5 or 1–3, but you can also use the descriptors that you have developed or simply categorise as VL, L, M, H, VH (for very low through to very high).

Proximity – You can record this either quantitatively, using days or weeks to impact, or simply as near, medium and far, or a variation of this approach.

Score – Whatever approach you take to scoring, record the score here. This is likely to be one of:
- a priority rank
- a RAG status or simple high-medium-low assessment
- a numerical combination of likelihood and impact
- a numerical combination of likelihood, impact and proximity.

Inherent Risk and Residual Risk

Some sophisticated risk registers record a base assessment of the inherent risk (should no mitigating actions be taken), and an assessment of the risk status (following mitigating actions), known as the residual risk.

In a less complex approach, your best method is to record your assessment of the risk as it is now. Once you have taken mitigating actions, revise your assessment and update your risk register accordingly. To maintain your audit trail, each time you make changes, change the version number or date stamp on the register, and keep a copy of the previous version as a record.

CHAPTER 6
PLAN FOR RISKS

ONCE YOU HAVE IDENTIFIED AND ANALYSED your project risks, and have a good understanding of the causes, triggers and consequences of each, you are ready to do something about them. As a project manager, however, you will not want to jump in feet first: you will want to develop plans.

This chapter will illustrate the six fundamental risk management strategies and describe how to use each to create the components of a total risk plan for your project. You will learn how to develop a Risk Action Plan for major risks and how to record your risk responses in your risk register.

When to do Risk Planning

If you try to complete your risk planning too early in the project's lifecycle, there is the possibility that you will be working with too little information and that your risk predictions will be inaccurate. This will give you perhaps the best start to your risk planning, but will require a lot of work that will need to be re-done as new information emerges.

If, on the other hand, you wait until you have a high degree of certainty, it is likely that some risks will already have matured, and some will involve greater cost to manage. Figure 6.1 illustrates this trade off and reminds us why most aspects of risk planning needs to happen during the planning stage of a project, while you will have started considering the major "project killer" threats back in the earliest definition stage of the project's lifecycle.

Figure 6.1: When to do Risk Planning

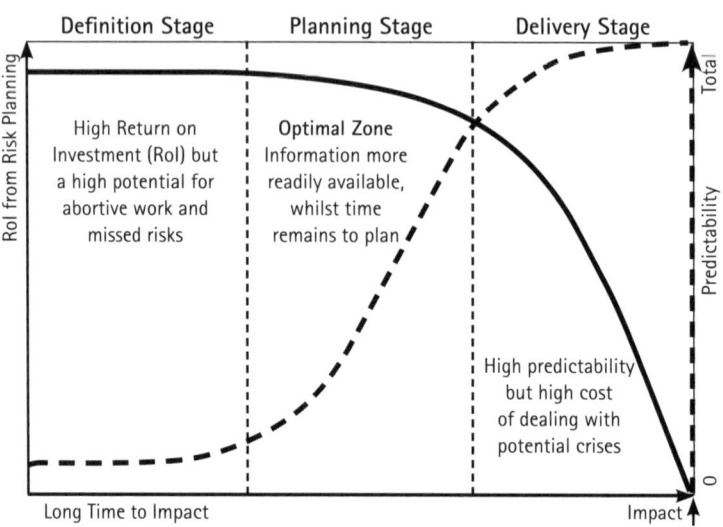

THE SIX FUNDAMENTAL STRATEGIES

The six fundamental strategies for managing project risk are:

1. Remove the risk
2. Reduce likelihood
3. Reduce impact
4. Contingency plan
5. Transfer risk
6. Accept the risk

For a significant, but not major risk, in what we identified as the "amber" zone in the previous chapter, one of these strategies is likely to be the basis of a satisfactory plan. As the likelihood and impact of a risk becomes greater, you will increasingly want to develop a plan based on multiple strategies, giving you a whole basket of approaches for the risks posing the greatest threat.

REMOVING THE RISK

The strongest approach to dealing with a risk is to remove it entirely, and the only certain way to do that is to not undertake the risky activity.

For example: the largest single source of accidental death in the UK in 2008 was caused by private motor vehicle accidents. In the US, firearms cause more deaths than motor vehicles. Let's consider the risk of a motor vehicle accident. We can avoid this risk entirely by staying at home and not going out, or we can remove the risk of accident in a private motor vehicle by using public transport or walking – both of which result in far fewer injuries and deaths.

In a project environment, Table 6.1 offers some examples of how you can implement this type of strategy.

Table 6.1: Tactics to Remove Project Risk

- **Over-design** – A "gold-plated" specification that is over-specified with respect to the core functionality. Examples include redundant components, over-size strength components or higher specification materials.
- **Buy certainty** – When you select components that are well tested, you can lock in certainty of functionality, quality or cost into a component of your plan. These are sometimes known as COTS ("Commercial Off-The-Shelf") solutions.
- **Alternative solution** – There may be other solutions to an element of your plan that offer complete certainty of schedule, budget or functionality.
- **Address root cause** – Root cause analysis, using techniques like the Fishbone and Five Whys (covered in Chapter 4), can help you identify a strategy that will address the cause and remove the threat.
- **Remove the risky element from your plan** – If you cannot control the risk and the threat level is unacceptable, you will need to remove that element from your plan and accept the compromise this causes.

At whole project level, this strategy means cancelling your project if the risk is not tolerable and no strategy will reduce it sufficiently. In some cases this may be your only option. However, when you review most published lists of risk avoidance tactics, you will find that the majority of suggestions are, in truth, ways to reduce the likelihood, rather than remove risk altogether.

REDUCING LIKELIHOOD

Continuing with the example of motor vehicle accidents, there are many ways to reduce the likelihood. These are the tactical elements of a plan:
- Drive less often
- Drive only when you feel fit and alert
- Choose the safest time of day to drive
- Pick your route carefully
- Turn off your mobile phone when driving
- Drive carefully, following the rules of the road
- Drive slowly

In the project management environment, Table 6.2 offers some strategies to reduce the likelihood of risk.

Table 6.2: Tactics to Reduce the Likelihood of Project Risk
- Visible, committed sponsorship.
- Effective communication of identified risks, project status, external events and new issues.
- Use of experts and specialists with relevant training and experience.
- A culture of openness and critical challenge.
- Effective monitoring and control processes.
- Follow established procedures that have been tested and certified where possible. Examples include quality processes, health and safety procedures, and workshop procedures.
- Project gateways and reviews, and assurance processes generally. There is more on project gateway reviews in Chapter 8.
- Involving stakeholders from day one, throughout your project.
- Establishing and following good decision-making processes with documented criteria, clarity of responsibility and access to all available data.
- Creating and evaluating prototypes and pilots and fully involving relevant stakeholders in the process.
- Allowing sufficient time and budget for testing and remediation.
- Minimising external dependencies and establishing effective communication and information-gathering where they exist.

REDUCE IMPACT

Many ways by which we reduce the impact of motor vehicle accidents – such as airbags, side impact protection, big and robust vehicles, and seatbelts – arguably increase the likelihood of accidents, as drivers feel increasingly safe and consequently more complacent when driving.

Driving slowly will reduce both the likelihood and impact of an accident. As a project manager, you have many tactics to reduce the impact of a risk.

Table 6.3: Tactics to Reduce the Impact of Project Risk
- Create plans with contingency in your budget, schedule, scope and quality. If there is none, or you use your contingency in your base plan, then any risk has the possibility of causing a cost or schedule over-run, or a loss of quality or functionality.
- Established procedures can reduce impact as well as likelihood, but in the event of problems, protective equipment and defensive procedures – such as a controlled shut down and fail-safe systems – can minimise damage.
- Where you can, ring fence activities, so that delays or problems in one area of your project have limited or no effect on other areas.
- Consider having redundancy in the development of critical parts of your project. If two teams are working independently to create the same piece of code or engineering component, then if one meets a hitch, the other will still deliver. This is expensive, but can be justified in the right circumstances.
- Rapid-cycle monitoring and control, with capacity for rapid response, can contain the damage from a risk. Many fire control systems do not reduce the likelihood of fire – they detect it early and deploy fire retardants or extinguishers rapidly.
- For risks such as theft or fraud, review stock levels and individual authorisations to balance risk and working efficiency.

One of the most important ways to reduce harm is to know what you will do if a risk becomes manifest. This is called a contingency plan.

CONTINGENCY PLAN

Contingency plans deal with the effects of a threat, rather than its causes. They are sometimes known as fall-back plans or as a plan B. A contingency plan will not make the risk any less likely to occur, nor make it any less harmful. However, it will give your team the means to deal with it immediately, with prepared systems, actions and resources. In our driver example, contingency plans include carrying a mobile phone and a list of numbers, having basic tools and a first aid kit in the car, maintaining a sound spare wheel and joining a roadside assistance scheme.

A contingency planning process is illustrated in Figure 6.2 and the steps are summarised in Table 6.4.

Figure 6.2: Contingency Planning Process

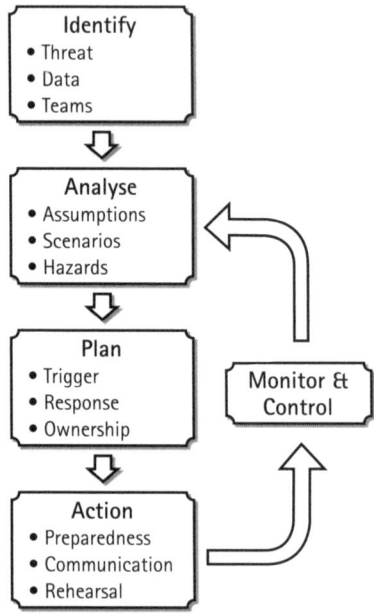

Table 6.4: Contingency Planning Process	
Identify	This is your preparation stage. Start with clarifying what threat or threats you are considering. Mobilise your contingency planning team and gather the information and data you need.
Analyse	Understand the hazards arising from the threat and identify suitable working assumptions. Develop a set of scenarios that cover the range of outcomes possible.
Plan	Define your objectives for the response – they may range from a minimum level of containment through to complete recovery. Your plan should cover the steps you will take, including how you will watch for triggering events. Define responsibilities and processes for management and coordination of the plan, and set out the resources (people, assets, materials) you will need. Finally, document your plan.
Action	This is about implementing preparedness by securing the resources you need, communicating your plan and where appropriate, rehearsing or testing the plan.
Monitor and control	Keep your plan under constant review, periodically re-evaluating the assumptions it is based on, checking resource availability and monitoring the situation for changes and triggering events.

Like any plan, your contingency plan will need an owner, who has ultimate responsibility for developing and maintaining the plan, scanning for trigger events, and taking charge in the event.

Table 6.5 sets out some typical components of a project risk contingency plan.

Table 6.5: Elements of a Contingency Plan for Project Risk

Schedule Contingency Plan
- Create a schedule contingency, or "float".
- Maintain surplus resources.
- Identify options for extended working hours.
- Look for non-dependent later activities that could be rescheduled.
- Identify non-critical activities that could be discarded.
- Identify non-critical deliverables that could be de-scoped by either dropping them or reducing functionality or quality criteria.
- Research ready-made solutions that could be bought in.
- Research ways of out-sourcing work or hiring contractors.
- Maintain one or more Tiger Teams – a highly capable, mixed-skill group that can be deployed to solve problems as they arise.

Budget Contingency Plan
- Create a budget contingency.
- Review resources allocations and identify non-critical people or stocks that could be released.
- Look at options to harness unpaid overtime working (extending the working day or week). This has risks of its own and is not appropriate in all project cultures. This is sometimes referred to as "sweating your assets".
- Identify non-critical activities, or deliverables, that you could de-scope, reducing functionality or quality criteria.

Functionality Failure Contingency Plan
- Build test and remediation time into your plans.
- Secure expert evaluators.
- Put in place effective change control procedures (see Chapter 8 for more details).

TRANSFER RISK

Driver's insurance does not reduce the likelihood or impact of an accident, but it will share the financial burden. Any contract between two parties will allocate the risk between them, so a well-drawn up contract will place each risk on the party who is best able to manage it cost effectively. Contracts are an essential part of project risk management. The four principle contractual mechanisms are:

1. Two parties agreeing to their respective contractual obligations: "I will do this if you do that."
2. Insurance: "You will pay me this if that happens."
3. Accepting a guarantee or an indemnity, or imposing a performance bond: "You will do that, or you must recompense me like this."

4. Imposing a disclaimer or waiver: "If that happens, I will not need to do this."

Risk transfer is most often applied to financial risks, but it can work equally well as a strategy to cope with schedule or performance risks.

Contracting Strategy

At whole project level, this strategy means creating a contract where a principal supplier or a group of contractors share substantial elements of project risk with the client. For big projects, with substantial amounts of procured goods or services, you will want to develop a strategy for how you will enter into contracts with your suppliers. At the one extreme (the more traditional end of the spectrum) you may seek to impose strict performance requirements on your suppliers, with whatever contractual incentives and penalties are available in your jurisdiction. At the other end, you may truly share some areas of risk with your suppliers, so that if certain risks manifest, you will work together to resolve them, with you taking ultimate responsibility.

As you move from the one end of the spectrum to the other, you can expect a less adversarial relationship, and also you should expect to pay less to your supplier. On the other hand, you do retain more risk.

ACCEPT THE RISK

Most of us who drive do so as carefully as we can, with the safest car we can afford, with roadside service phone numbers, mobile phones, spares in our car and insurance paid up. Even so, we know that every time we start a journey, there is a chance we won't end it. We accept the risk. We do so because the price of reducing the risk further is too great and thus not acceptable – the benefits of mobility outweigh the risks.

It would be wrong to simply accept the risk blindly, with no consideration of the scale of threat, nor of its consequences, or because, like some foolish drivers, you believe that there is no real threat. However, if you consider the risk carefully, and consider the threat small enough and your options for mitigation are not cost effective, then accepting the risk is an appropriate and deliberate strategy.

You may argue that this is no different from the strategy of having a contingency plan. The distinction is that in this strategy, you will deal with the effects after risk materialises with no prior preparation; it is a wholly reactive strategy.

This does not, however, remove the need to constantly monitor the situation. We drive with our eyes open! This "accept and monitor" approach is sometimes falsely referred to as a "passive response". It must not be. Make your monitoring all the more active, because if you don't have a plan, you will need to react very quickly!

At "whole project" level, this strategy means knowingly pursuing a high-risk project despite the total risk level, because the rewards or the imperative outweigh that risk.

MORE RESEARCH

Sometimes, you cannot form a satisfactory plan with the information you have at your disposal – perhaps you are at too early a stage in your project lifecycle, as illustrated in Figure 6.1. If this is the case, your approach will be to do more research. This is not a distinct or separate strategy, but recognition that you need more information to develop a plan.

Figure 6.3: More Research in your Risk Management Process

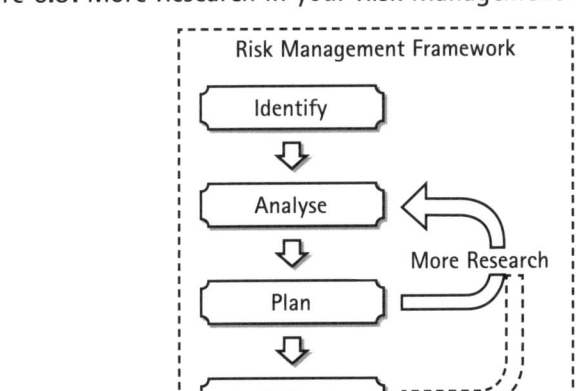

RESPONDING TO OPPORTUNITIES

So far in this chapter we have treated all risks as threats. It is time to consider, briefly, how you can plan to respond to opportunities, should they manifest. There are three main strategies:

- **Enhancing the likelihood** – Look for ways that you can foster opportunities and make them more likely to emerge. Pasteur's saying, "fortune favours the prepared mind", suggests that if you know what opportunities you seek, you can take steps to increase your chances of getting them.
- **Enhancing the impact** – How can you improve on the gains that an opportunity offers? If you finish a project stage early, you may be able to make savings, advance other work and improve functionality!
- **Knowing it when you see it** – If you are not prepared, then you may not be ready to seize the opportunities that come your way, and exploit them for the project's benefit – or for the benefit of your client.

RISK RESPONSE PLAN

You will not always need an individual plan for particular risks, but when you do encounter major risks on a large project, you may want to document them on a Risk Response Plan. Table 6.6 sets out some typical components.

Table 6.6: Risk Response Plan*	
Section 1: The Risk	Risk title Unique risk ID number Risk description Project elements affected (usually by reference to your WBS) Risk originator Risk owner
Section 2: Risk Analysis	Trigger Likelihood Impact Proximity/time scale Score *more >>>*

Section 3: Risk Response	Actions Timing/schedule Resources (people, assets, materials) Responsibilities Communication process Reporting Budget
Section 4: Residual Risk	Residual risk Monitoring processes Contingency arrangements
Section 5: Authorisation	Sign-off Version control *You can download a sample template from www.riskhappens.co.uk

RISK REGISTER: RECORDING PLANS AND ASSIGNING RESPONSIBILITIES

Your risk register is as much a planning and monitoring tool as a document of record, so you will use it to document your action plan for each risk. The basic components of this aspect of your risk register are illustrated by Table 6.7.

Table 6.7: Risk Register – Part 3

...	Risk Management Plan	Owner	Planned Dates		...
			Next Review	Target Completion	

Risk Management Plan – Use this section to record your plan. If you have multiple elements to your plan, and are using a spreadsheet, then consider having several rows devoted to your risk, so that you can track each element of your plan seperately. Likewise, if you are creating a risk register database, you may want to consider allowing each plan to occupy a table of its own.

Owner – The minimum reasonable requirement for assigning personnel to risks on your risk register is to ensure each risk has an owner: someone who has final responsibility for planning your response, ensuring it gets carried out and monitoring the status of the risk. You may also want space to allocate additional personnel to the risk, in other specific or general roles. As project manager, resist the temptation to make yourself risk owner on too many risks. Not only could this easily overload you, but it also means you have no one to chase or, put another way, the risk owners have nobody to chase them!

Next Review – This is the date when you will next review the status of the risk, progress on your risk management plan and its effectiveness.

Target Completion – This is the date when you plan to have all actions on your risk management plan completed. This may or may not be the point at which you will be able to close out the risk as posing no residual threat.

CHAPTER 7
TAKE ACTION ON RISKS

EXPERIENCED PROJECT MANAGERS are sometimes called upon to review other projects. At one of these reviews, I moved onto the subject of risk: "Tell me what you are doing about risk," I asked. The project manager was well prepared and showed me a printout of a splendid risk register. I was suitably impressed, and passing back the printout, I repeated: "So, tell me what you are doing about risk..." Looking slightly embarrassed, as if perhaps I'd missed the significance of the documents, the project manager slid them back to me across the table. "Oh yes, these are great. Now, tell me what you are *doing* about risk..."

A plan is nothing without action. Often, we unconsciously think that once we have planned for risk, the universe will get to hear about it and will mysteriously prevent the risk from happening. It won't. Your risk register is more than a record – it's a management tool, so use it to manage.

RISK MANAGEMENT PROCESS

The need for action is not *just* a step in our four-step process. After you have gone through the process once and are starting to revisit your plan, it should suffuse each of the steps.

Figure 7.1: Take Action on Risks

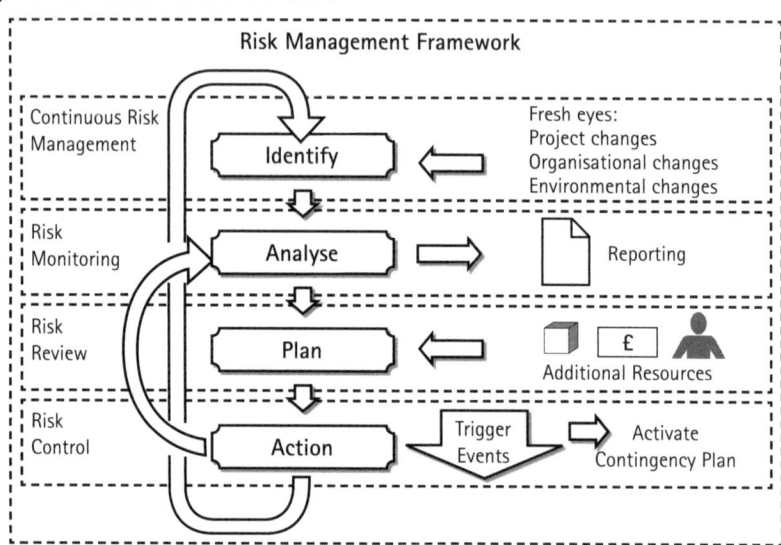

The action step itself arises from implementing your plan. It must also involve actively scanning the environment for trigger events or emerging issues. If a trigger event does occur, then you will need to activate a contingency plan.

Continuous risk management means not just analysing the outcomes of the actions you take, but also undertaking regular reviews to identify new risks emerging from changes in your project, the organisation and the wider environment. When you can, bring in fresh eyes, rather than rely solely on team members who have been around for a while and may not be able to see some of the obvious risks.

RISK OR ISSUE?

Before looking at your risk management routine, and how your risk register can support you in this step of the risk management process, it is worth clarifying the important distinction between a risk and an issue. The difference is uncertainty: risk is used to describe uncertain factors that can affect outcomes. An issue is something that *will* happen, or indeed, *has* happened. An issue is something that has to be dealt with.

RISK MANAGEMENT ROUTINE

The keys to getting this step right are persistence and routine. There are a number of different routines you can adopt, some complementing one another, some working well on their own. Decide which routines will work well for you, on your project, with your challenges and resources. Introduce the routine, test it and modify it as you learn what works best.

Routine 1: Risk Register Review

On one project I managed, risk was my key lever to project success. So at the start of each morning, I reviewed the risk register and made a list of half a dozen risks I wanted to see progress on. I then spent the rest of the morning working with risk owners to support, cajole, advise, debrief and generally push them forward.

As project manager, get into the habit of regularly scanning your risk register and reviewing elements of it in detail with the risk owners. This approach illustrates one of the benefits of using a spreadsheet over a simple table: the ability to sort and filter. One morning, you can print all the risks for which Chris is the risk owner; on another, you can print all of the risks linked to a particular work-stream; and again, you could review all of the risks that have not been reviewed in the last fortnight.

Once you have a cut of your risk register, giving you a list of risks to review today, make the time to speak with the individual risk owners to check on their progress, update on risk status, and challenge them to ensure that current plans are still relevant. Make notes so that you can update your risk register following the meeting. Holding risk owners to account in this way is an important part of your role as a project manager.

Routine 2: Morning Stand-ups

At one project I worked on, all of the managers would get together to drink a cup of coffee and discuss the coming day's challenges at around 8:30 am. By the end of the coffee, we could coordinate our work and had discussed how to resolve tricky problems that were emerging.

This approach has become more widely used in recent years, due to the increasing popularity of "agile" project management methods, which originated in the software development arena. Now, these ideas are being used in a wide variety of projects and the regular 15 minute all-hands stand-up meeting is a common feature of many projects. In agile project environments, it is also known as a "roll-call meeting" or a "scrum".

Project managers have been using this approach for years – possibly back to the Pharaohs' pyramid builders. Sometimes, the meeting is for everyone on the project; sometimes for key participants or team leaders. The focus is on the daily plan: what people achieved yesterday, what they commit to achieving today, and most important for us, what obstacles they face. By writing these on a board, the whole team can gain a shared understanding of the current risks and issues.

As routine and discipline are important, it helps to keep these meetings short (hence standing up) and at a regular time and place each day. Keep the energy up and the time down by asking each participant for headlines, not stories. If you want to use this mechanism to focus on risks rather than progress, four good questions to ask are:

1. What progress did you make on project risks yesterday?
2. What progress do you plan to make today?
3. What new risks or emerging issues have you become aware of since yesterday?
4. What obstacles do you foresee?

Outside the meeting, team members can get together to resolve the obstacles.

Routine 3: Working Group

On one project I led, a great number of risks and issues required high-level intervention from the client organisation. So twice a month, a group of second tier operational directors would meet for an hour. Over a coffee, I would get from each person a list of pressing topics and list them on a board. As we sat down, we prioritised the list. We would then work briskly through the list in priority order, deciding on what action was needed and who would deal with it. With five minutes to go, we marked initials against any outstanding items on the list, and that person would then initiate off-line discussions as necessary.

This "kitchen cabinet" style of leadership works well when you want to harness the energy and authority of senior people to clear paths and resolve risks on a project. It allows greater depth of discussion than a morning stand-up, but the dynamic way that the team builds and prioritises its agenda will ensure that the most important topics are always dealt with.

Routine 4: Risk Language in Every Conversation

As a project manager, I like to think I have a great team, committed to a great plan. So what can go wrong? Always keep risks at the forefront of your conversations with team members, sponsors, clients and other stakeholders. Even when everything is going well, new risks emerge – sometimes as the unintended consequence of treating an existing risk.

Figure 7.2: Consequential Risks Arise from Treating an Existing Risk

Routine 5: Constant Communication

In Chapter 8 we will cover formal project risk reporting and in Chapter 10 we will turn to the less formal involvement of stakeholders. Both of these elements contribute to an essential part of any project's routine: relentless communication. Use your knowledge of the prevailing cultures to establish regular and ad hoc communications that ensure everyone knows what the risks are, and their role in addressing them; also ensure that you, or your risk manager if you have one, get to hear about any new risks that somebody identifies.

RISK REGISTER: DEALING WITH PROGRESS AND CLOSING DOWN RISKS

The final section of our basic risk register records progress and final status.

Table 7.1: Risk Register – Part 4					
...	Risk Management Progress		Risk Closure		...
	Status	Date	Status	Date	

Risk Management Progress – Record the status of your plans and the progress you have made, and also the date of your most recent review.

Risk Closure – A risk on your register may be "open" (ongoing) or it may be "closed" (completed). If it is open, it is still a threat (or opportunity), but when closed, you are stating that the risk can no longer affect the project outcome. Record the date of risk closure.

There are four reasons why you may close a risk:

1. **Deleted**

    Your description of the risk encompasses two or more risks, so you delete it and replace it by new risks in your risk register. Remember that to ensure the integrity of your audit trail, you must not re-use the unique risk ID.

2. **Completed**
The risk response has been completed and there is no or negligible residual risk.

3. **Outdated**
The risk is no longer a threat or opportunity, either because it never really was, or because the possibility of the triggering event has expired, or because the causal circumstances have changed.

4. **Occurred**
The risk has materialised and been dealt with as an issue or the benefit realised.

CHAPTER 8
RISK MONITORING AND CONTROL

THE MONITOR AND CONTROL LOOP is the beating heart of project management during the delivery phase, and equally, at the core of your risk management process. Project monitoring and control covers a broad range of things, including schedule, budget, resource utilisation, delivery, quality, variances and more. Risk must assume an equal place on this list.

Figure 8.1: Risk Monitoring and Control

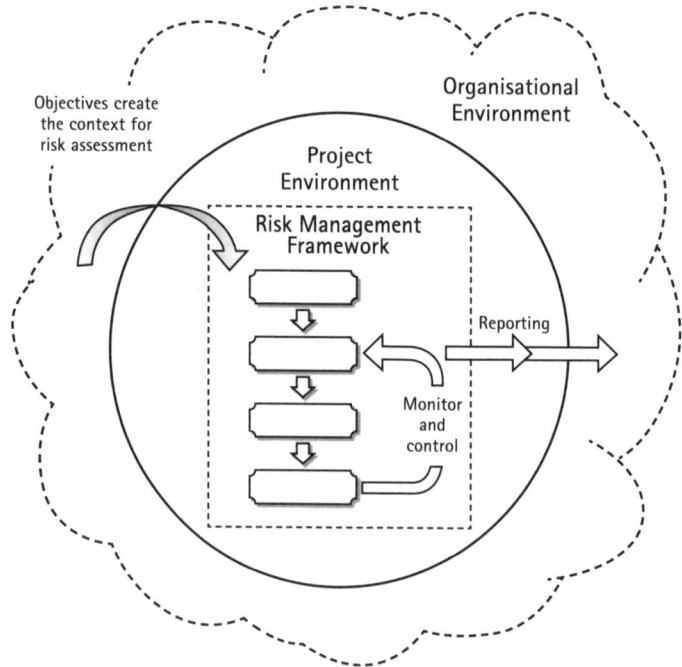

MONITORING

Perhaps the "gold standard" of project monitoring techniques is Earned Value Analysis (EVA) or Earned Value Management (EVM). It is beyond the scope of this book to describe this in detail (beyond the illustration in Figure 8.2). If you are working on a major project, it is worth evaluating the benefits of adopting this robust and rigorous approach against the undoubted overhead it imposes in its set-up and data-gathering requirements.

EVA starts with a detailed assessment of the work to be done. This is scheduled and budgeted, and the planned rate of committing expenditure is plotted to give a cost versus time graph, with your plan represented by the line marked BCWS – Budget Cost of Work Scheduled. As work proceeds, two further curves will give you valuable insights: the Actual Cost of Work Performed (ACWP), which tells you the true expenditure; and the Budget Cost of Work Performed (BCWP), which tells you how much you planned to spend on the work. Figure 8.2 shows you how you can measure your performance against budget and schedule, from these three curves.

Figure 8.2: Earned Value Analysis

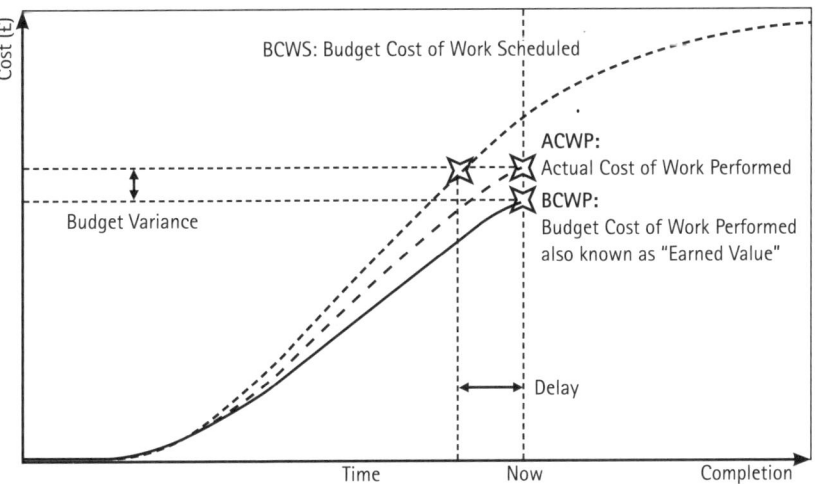

For all projects, however, you should be identifying key progress measures and monitoring against them on a regular cycle that is frequent enough to allow you to spot problems when they are still small, and identify risk triggers early on.

Where you find a difference between your planned progress measure and the actual situation, you need to understand the risks involved and the causes. If it is a positive variance, what are the opportunities, and how can you foster more of this enhanced performance level? For adverse variances, what are the threats and how can you avoid a repeat of this slippage in future? Also keep in mind that your project is an interconnected network of people, activities and schedules, which means that one variance may very well trigger others.

The Warning Signs

Table 8.1 sets out some common indicators of problems to come.

Table 8.1: Leading Indicators of Project Risk	
Schedule risk	• Minor milestones being missed • Forecasts of late milestone delivery • Unclear answers to direct questions about schedule • Meetings cancelled or rescheduled • Planned trades union action • Schedule contingencies being used or exceeded
Budget risk	• Rate-of-spend variances against budget • Rate-of-spend variances against completion level or product delivery • Contractor claims for contract variations • Change requests • Unplanned changes in supplier/contractor/consultant staff numbers • Economic indicators turn down, affecting sponsoring organisation • Budget contingencies being used or exceeded
Performance risk	• Staff absence rates • General staff welfare and morale • Staff turnover • Adverse news coverage of contractor or supplier
Scope risk	• New stakeholders emerging • New technology becoming available • New industry trends *more >>>*

Quality risk	• Schedule squeeze with no requests for time extensions • Component failures • Poor quality of interim deliverables
Governance risk	• Absence of sponsor or project board members from scheduled meetings • High level personnel changes in the sponsoring organisation • Project board meetings fail to address material matters • Project board meetings focus is at an inappropriately detailed level • A lack of concern at senior level for significant risks

REPORTING

The whole process of preparing a formal project report should be "bottom-up" – that is, starting with raw data, analysing it to draw conclusions and then summarising and abstracting it to the required level of detail. Risk reporting is one part of the overall project picture.

Low-level Risk Reporting: The Detail

At the most detailed level, you may want to report on the status of individual risks, line by line, possibly focusing on high (red status) or high and medium (red and amber status) priority risks. This is often accompanied by a scatter plot showing the location of each risk on a two-dimensional chart of likelihood against impact.

Figure 8.3: Risk Reporting – Scatter Plot

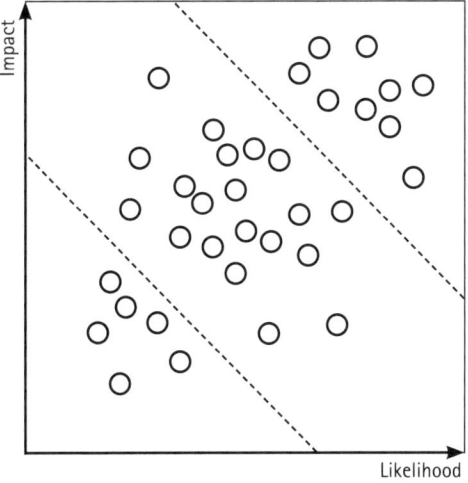

Mid-level Risk Reporting: The Story

At this level, your representation of risk status will be more abstract and focus on trends and patterns. Figure 8.4 illustrates how you can report on the time trend of risks at red status (top priority), showing total number of open risks, and total number of former red status risks either reduced to green status (low priority) or blue status (closed). You can adapt this approach to report on whatever is of most relevance to your project. For example: threats emerging, risks closed, total number of threats or opportunities or threats manifesting.

Figure 8.4: Risk Reporting – Trend Analysis

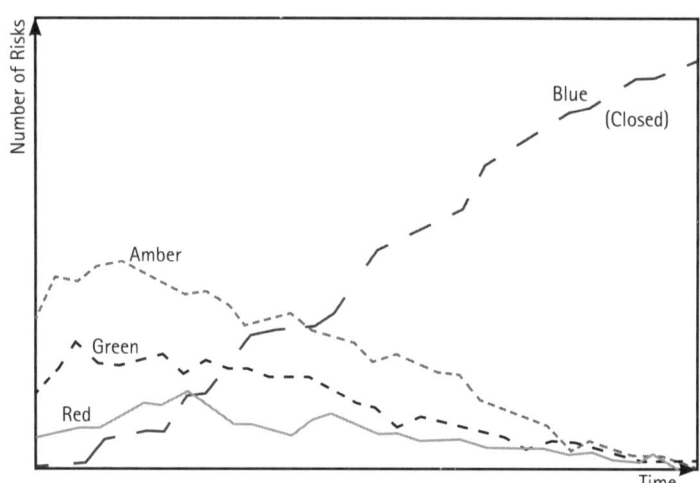

Figure 8.5 reveals the pattern of risks. Once you have a useful classification for your risks, this "radar plot" or "spidergram" allows you to see the total number of risks (or the number or high priority risks) in each category. This shows clearly where the risks lie on your project.

Figure 8.5: Risk Reporting – Category Analysis

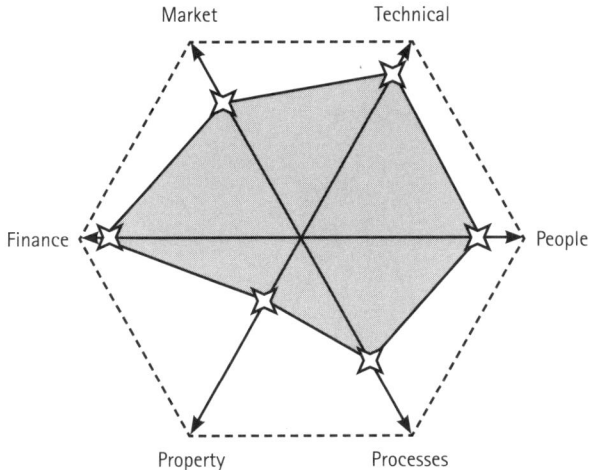

High-level Risk Reporting: The Headlines

At the highest level, you may only need to report two things:
1. The number and change since the last report of the highest level risks.
2. The nature of threat and remedial actions for the few major risks.

CONTROL: DEALING WITH PROBLEMS

We monitor so that we can control. When you encounter a threat or an opportunity, apply the SCOPE method to the problem:

Stop – Don't react instantly: take time to compose yourself and consider what you have learned.

Clarify – Where you need to, gather information to be sure you understand the situation fully.

Options – Develop a number of options, then evaluate which one offers the greatest chance of success.

Proceed – Now act on your preferred action decisively.

Evaluate – Ensure you assess the outcomes and your process so that you can learn from the experience, whether it was a success or not.

Time, Cost, Quality and Scope

Most problems can be better understood by reference to the four corners of the time-cost-quality-scope tetrahedron.

Figure 8.6: Time-Cost-Quality-Scope

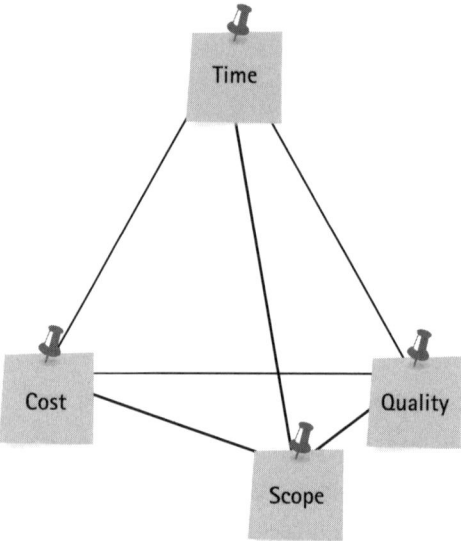

First, this will help you understand where your project priorities lay and the extent to which the problem challenges that priority. Second, it shows where you can fruitfully look for a solution. Let's take an example.

In a project to develop a new financial system, the daily reporting module is causing the developers problems. The project manager's sponsor, the finance director, is adamant that the quality of the data must not be compromised, while the Board has set a rigid deadline for implementation of this system, as a key enabler to other changes that will meet their commitments to shareholders.

This means that the project manager has two levers to pull: scope or cost. The options are either to invest more money and resources into remedying the problem, or negotiate a controlled change with the sponsor to reduce the scope of functionality of the daily reporting module. A careful analysis of these two options means that the project manager can offer the sponsor a clear choice, with costs and consequences.

Crashing the Timeline

If things go wrong, you may need to make up a significant amount of time. If you are prepared to make compromises to do so, this is called "crashing the timeline". It usually involves loading extra resources, rather than compromising quality or scope. This means that you will trade extra cost for time gained, and may also add new types of risks in exchange for reducing schedule risk.

The ideas in Table 8.2 show the range of trade-offs that can be available for you to choose from; the columns do not form prescriptions for operating procedures. Particularly beware of adding new people at the last minute into a late-running project. You can find that the time taken in resolving their queries about "what", "how" and even "why" can affect productivity and even morale within an already over-worked team. If you do bring new people in, focus them on particular areas of the project where they can quickly be productive with a focused brief. Their fresh viewpoint might otherwise mean that their well-meaning challenges to plans, work done or working practices can disrupt the team when it least needs it.

Table 8.2: Crashing the Timeline			
	Normal job	Rush job	Crash job
Defining the outcome	Absolute clarity	Absolute clarity	Absolute clarity
Defining the task/s	Clear task definition	Tasks take pragmatic route	Anything goes to achieve outcome
Agreeing a solution	Consensus and sign-off	Sign-off	Discussion sufficient to create trust
Planning the process	Full, detailed plan	Gaps in detail tolerated	Framework plan + instinct/experience
Other workload	Integrate project around other tasks	Project tasks prioritised	Everything else put aside

more >>>

Use of resources	Use of resources balanced against budgetary priorities	Additional resources secured; bring in experts and a Tiger Team (see Table 6.5)	All available resources called in and deployed; extended working hours, overtime and weekends
Budget	Careful management of budget	Some additional spending authorised	Cost priorities subordinated – base level cost control only
Premium services	For example: limited use of things like overnight delivery	For example: frequent use of things like overnight delivery	For example: overnight delivery becomes the norm
Risk-taking	Optimised	Additional calculated risks accepted	Significant risks accepted
Attitude	focus – Get the job done	JDI – Just Do It! Single-minded focus	JFDI! Tunnel vision
Recreation time	Plenty of recreation time	Some loss of recreation time	Late nights and early mornings; stress levels and physical/mental condition monitored

Re-baselining

If you have ever been driving around an unfamiliar area and taken a wrong turn, you may know what it feels like to have driven off the edge of your map. You pull over in a small village and have two choices:

1. You could turn the car around, drive in circles, look out for landmarks, and hope you find yourself back on the map.
2. You could ask a local where you are and then go and buy a new map.

If the choice seems obvious (and it should), then why is it that so many project managers will push on with a failing project in the hope that a miracle will happen and they will get back on plan before disaster strikes?

If shift happens and your plan is no longer a good guide to what the future holds, then stop your project – or only allow activities to continue if you are highly confident that they are right. Use your people to re-plan the project from an accurate assessment of where you are. This fundamental re-planning to deal with unexpected events is called "re-baselining". It will give you a new plan from which to monitor and control your project and thus bring a greater level of confidence going forward. Usually, the time you divert into the planning process would have easily been wasted in casting around without a plan.

CONTROL: SCOPE AND QUALITY CHANGES
One of the most important tools for containing risk is the change control process. You will inevitably encounter requests for changes during the life of your project and part of your role as project manager is to deal with them. It is equally inappropriate to say "no" to all change requests as it is to say "yes". What you need is a process to evaluate each request fully and refer it to the right decision maker or body.

Request for Change
Once a need for a change is identified, the person who wants to make the change will make a "request for change". On a small project, this may be via a conversation or an email: on larger projects, this will be done more formally. On large projects, the project manager will usually appoint somebody into the role of change controller.

The role of the change controller is to ensure all proposed changes are recorded, fully reviewed and either accepted, deferred or rejected by an authorised person (or group, such as a project board). The request for change should include:
- details of the proposed change
- the reasons for the change and benefits of adopting it.

Evaluation and Approval/Rejection/Deferral
Before a proposed change can be considered, it needs to be reviewed and all relevant information and implications assessed. This assessment should include:
- Work/Product Breakdown Structure elements affected by the change
- Budget/cost impact
- Schedule/time impact
- Resource requirement

- Impact on other projects/activities
- Risks created by accepting the change

On projects where you can anticipate a large amount of change requests (for example, a complex and innovative project), consider establishing a "change authority" group with the power to review and approve or reject all change requests up to a certain size, on behalf of the project board. On a small project, approval or rejection of a proposed change may occur orally or by email. On a larger project, the person or group that approved the original business case will consider the proposal and review it, to determine whether the proposed change is:

- beneficial to the project (in which case it will *approve* the change request – with or without modification)
- not beneficial to the project (in which case it will *reject* the change request)
- inadequately assessed or pending further information (in which case it will *defer* the change request).

If you anticipate a significant number of change requests on your project, it is worth establishing systems at the outset, which might include:

- A *change log* to record all change requests, the approval status, and progress with the change. It might also include an incremental budget, to help with your financial audit trail.
- A delegated *change authority* – a person or group authorised to consider and approve or reject change requests on behalf of the sponsor or board.
- A *standard change request form* that itemises the information that the decision makers will need, to assess the request.
- Documented *criteria* for acceptance, rejection or deferral.
- A published *calendar* of dates when change requests are considered, which is frequent enough to ensure prompt attention.

You can download sample templates for a change request and change log document from *www.riskhappens.co.uk*.

CONTROL: TAKING ADVANTAGE OF OPPORTUNITIES

Sometimes you will have an opportunity to create the same deliverables with a smaller budget, fewer resources or in less time, or to create superior deliverables with the time and resources at your disposal.

Technology projects often offer such opportunities, because while you are working on a solution rooted in the technology that was available during the definition stage of your project, new technologies may be emerging and maturing to a point where they represent a real advantage in your application. Long-cycle military procurements are particularly prone to this happening.

Seizing the opportunity to re-cast your project can be a difficult decision. You may need to write off completed work and accept a delay (and maybe more cost), to achieve a better product, which is faster, more reliable, more flexible or more effective. Making this decision for the good of the sponsoring organisation requires a robust change control process with genuinely objective decision making.

You may also encounter opportunities to reduce budget or accelerate the project with better equipment, shortcuts, expert contributions or simple good luck. Taking up these opportunities is regarded as good project management rather than "opportunity management". These opportunities rarely come to you out of the blue, however. Stay attuned to them by talking with and listening to team members and maintaining an open attitude. Creative ideas often come unbidden from the least expected places. Reading widely and visiting other projects can provide the stimulation you need to spot an opportunity that has lain dormant for a long time.

RISK ASSURANCE

Risk assurance is a formal process for assessing the project team's handling of risk: the team's identification and assessment processes, the quality of its planning and decision making and the effectiveness of its implementation of mitigation or contingency plans. Four processes contribute to risk assurance:

1. Internal Risk Review

Internal risk reviews are led by the project manager or risk manager and supplement the day-to-day risk management processes. These rarely look at the process, but focus on the risks themselves. There are two components to the review:

- **Current risks**

    Review the status of the risk, its plans and actions taken. Ensure ownership and accountabilities are clear and that satisfactory progress is being made towards reducing the risk to an acceptable level.

- **New risks**

    Identify new risks to the project and begin the process of assessing them and assigning ownership.

The internal risk review will lead to a comprehensive update of your risk register.

2. Project Board Scrutiny

As a part of its overall project scrutiny, the project board or steering group will sometimes want to examine your risk management process. Their strategic remit will mean that they should confine themselves at first to the process and an examination of major and strategic level risks. If they do find shortcomings, they should then instigate a deeper review that examines the detail.

3. Risk Audits

These externally led risk reviews focus on the risk management process. The auditors may be unqualified to assess the plans you have made, but will be trained to evaluate:
- the suitability of your risk management processes
- the extent to which they are being followed.

A poor plan may not show up in this process (but should become apparent in an internal risk review), but if that plan is not being actioned or monitored, then that weakness will be noted.

4. Gateways

Good project governance demands that a project must not be able to continue from inception to closure without checks that it should move from one stage to the next. These checks are known as *gateways*, *gates* or *stage-gates*. The metaphor is obvious: to proceed, the project team must cross a barrier.

At these gateways, the team must answer two fundamental questions. How these questions are framed will depend upon the stage of the project:
- Has the project completed everything it must complete at this stage, to be considered ready to move on?
- If so, is it good for the organisation for the project to move to the next stage, and commit the next tranche of expenditure, resources and time?

Projects only proceed through the gateway if the answer to both questions is "yes". Part of a gateway review will always be a consideration of risk. This should include an assessment of whether risk levels are fully understood and are acceptable, and whether the risk process is sufficient to manage the project risks in the future stages. The gateway decision is fundamentally a risk decision:

> *If we make the investment required of us by the project (in terms of resources, money and time), do we have sufficient confidence that the project will produce an overall beneficial outcome that outweighs the cost?*

In this gateway decision, we can see both elements of risk: uncertainty and outcome. Some project management processes, such as the UK Government's PRINCE 2 methodology, embed the gateway process at the heart of project governance. Whether you are compelled to do so or not, this approach is a valuable part of risk management.

CHAPTER 9
RISK RESILIENCE

RESILIENCE IS YOUR ABILITY TO COPE with adverse events and recover from them. What makes resilience to risk so demanding is the observation that risks tend not to be additive, but multiplicative. The effects of a new risk seem to compound the problems of the last one to manifest; it does seem that once one risk has hit, others will surely follow: risks are rarely truly independent, even if they seem so.

> *When sorrows come, they come not single spies but in battalions.*
>
> Claudius, King of Denmark (from Hamlet by William Shakespeare)

Three levels of planning for these challenges are relevant to the project environment:
- scenario planning
- contingency planning
- business continuity planning.

While each would merit a book of its own, we will explore the essentials of each in turn.

SCENARIO PLANNING

Scenarios are stories about how your project might unfold. They consider how three particular elements can interact to create a range of possible futures, or scenarios. These three things are:

1. The current situation, which can be known with high confidence levels.
2. The driving forces for change, which can be known with middle confidence levels.
3. Future events, which can be known with lowest confidence levels.

Figure 9.1: Scenario Analysis

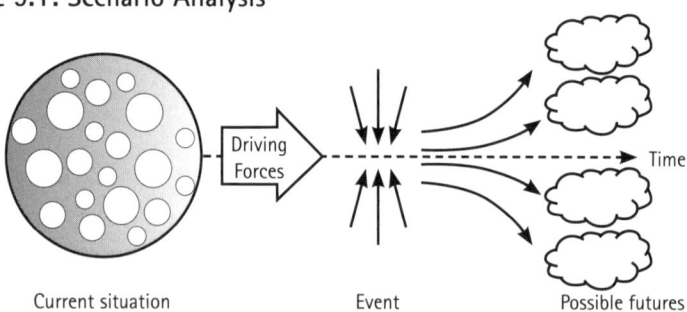

The basic process for scenario planning is illustrated in Figure 9.2. Look at your basket of predicted risks (you can't work with them all, so take a biggish selection) and look at scenarios of several risks manifesting. What would you do? You need processes, plans and resources.

Figure 9.2: Scenario Planning

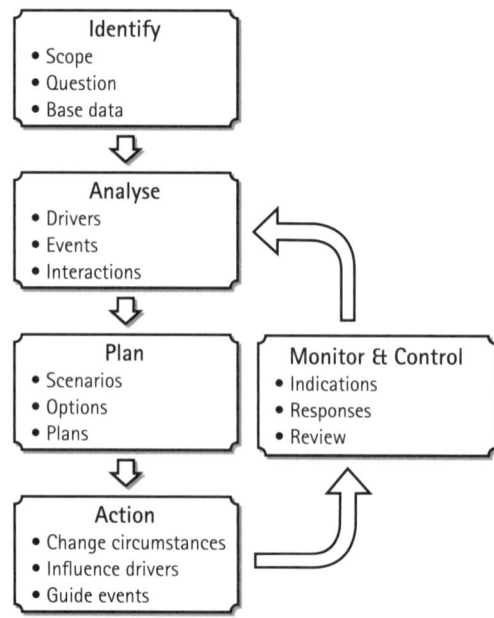

Table 9.1: Scenario Planning Process

Identify	Start by understanding the question you want to answer: what time frame, what areas of the project, what risks? Once you have decided, gather any useful data, forecasts and opinions.
Analyse	Now it is time to identify the drivers for change and the possible future events that will interact with one another and the current situation to create your scenarios. Tools that were discussed in Chapter 4, such as brainstorming, brainwriting and the Delphi method, are useful for scenario planning.
Plan	There are an infinite number of possible "micro-scenarios", so distil these into 3–5 broad principal scenarios that capture the essence of each type. These should range from an optimistic to a plausible worst case. For each one explore your options and put together plans for how you will respond. The next section of this chapter discusses contingency planning in more detail.
Action	The actions you take will be designed to do one or more of three things: • Change current circumstances • Influence the drivers for change • Predict and guide events
Monitor and control	Continually scan the project for indicators of where scenario changes may be moving events. Respond accordingly and periodically review your analysis and plans.

CONTINGENCY PLANNING

Contingency planning determines what we do about each scenario (see Chapter 6 for a more in depth discussion). For risk resilience, you need to apply that approach to scenarios that involve multiple risks. This can lead to a significant event that might be described as a "crisis" or a "disaster". These can threaten your whole organisation and its ability to deliver the products or services that define its business.

This leads us to the key question of how contingency planning relates to business continuity planning, disaster recovery and crisis management:

Business continuity (BC) addresses an organisation's ability to maintain operations and continue to deliver products and services to its customers following a disruptive event. It assumes that prevention has not been possible and that an incident has interrupted normal business and corrective action is necessary.

Disaster recovery (DR) is how an organisation will recover use of its critical technology infrastructure and data after a disruptive event. DR focuses on systems and data, whilst BC focuses on the whole operations. DR is therefore a component of BC.

Crisis management is how an organisation deals with a disruptive event that threatens to harm the organisation, its stakeholders or the general public. It focuses on the communications process: what to say, how to say it and who will say it. Three elements are common to most definitions of crisis: a threat to the organisation; the element of surprise; and a short decision time to respond.

BUSINESS CONTINUITY

Few projects will have the capacity to disrupt the operations of either the organisation that is sponsoring it or delivering it. However, if yours is one of them, then your scenario analysis must identify this possibility and you must plan for it.

Your organisation will almost certainly have a team responsible for business continuity, so make contact immediately and open a dialogue. They will have the experience and skills to understand your scenario and guide you in any actions you need to take. Figure 9.3 illustrates the basic business continuity management process.

Figure 9.3: Business Continuity Management

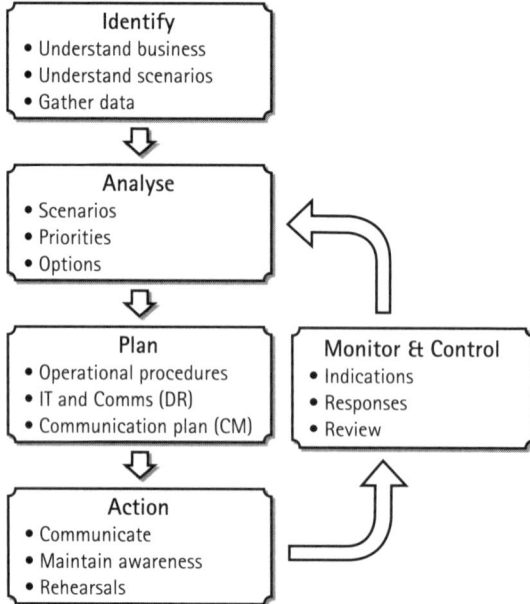

Table 9.2: Business Continuity Management Process

Identify	Understand your business context, its strategic and operational priorities and the scenarios that can impact upon it. Gather information about high priority operational processes and key customers, suppliers, partners and regulators.
Analyse	Play out the scenarios to determine how they will affect your business priorities and therefore understand what processes, systems and assets you will need to prioritise in your business continuity (BC) plan. Devise and cost the options.
Plan	Develop a business continuity plan that covers staffing, operations, IT and communications infrastructure and data, and both internal and external communications.
Action	Communicate your BC plan and create wide awareness of its spirit and detail. Everyone must know their roles under each scenario. Rehearse the plan and test it in all areas.
Monitor and control	Continually scan events for indications of change. Respond accordingly and periodically review your analysis and plans.

CHAPTER 10
INVOLVING STAKEHOLDERS IN RISK MANAGEMENT

A STAKEHOLDER IS ANYONE who has an interest in your project: they may be affected by its process or outcome, or they may be able to affect its outcome. Your stakeholders will determine the success – or not – of your project.

Stakeholders are both a source of risk on your project and also a resource that can help you manage the risks. Whilst stakeholder management is a project discipline in itself, any understanding of risk management must at least incorporate the basics of stakeholder management.

STAKEHOLDERS AS A SOURCE OF RISK

Projects naturally introduce change. Whilst anybody who can easily see a personal gain from that change will immediately support it, others will naturally react against that change. You must therefore anticipate the threat of resistance and plan for how you will deal with it.

Resistance is not always a deliberate campaign: it is often preceded by an uncomfortable period of emotional responses, followed by a period of adjustment. Understanding how people will respond to change that they perceive as adverse is essential for any project manager. Here is a description of five typical stages.

Table 10.1: The Stages of Resistance to Change	
Denial	Before a threat activates someone's "fight or flight" reflex, people often experience a short period of "fright" when they freeze. In the context of change, there is a period when we tell ourselves that the change won't happen, or if it does, it won't affect me, or if it does, it won't be for a while. It is our brain's way of giving us time to adjust.
Emotion	Once our brain accepts that there is a threat (real or imagined), it reacts first at an emotional level – we can become angry, upset, fearful, frustrated, bitter, or any combination of these and other emotions. Not everyone shows them of course.
Resistance	As our brain further processes the situation, the rational parts become involved and we start to find objections to the change. This is resistance.
Adjustment	If the argument for change is strong, then we will start to evaluate and then entertain those arguments, moving towards a reasoned acceptance of the change.
Acceptance	Real acceptance requires one more shift: to an emotional readiness to change. If there is a significant benefit to us, we may even move into a state of commitment to supporting the change.

When changes occur, the responses of your stakeholders can therefore disrupt the project, unless you have a plan in place to deal with the range of responses that you can reasonably predict. As your project nears completion, some of your stakeholders will need to be prepared for new ways of working, following the adoption of the new processes, systems, technology or assets into their workplace. Failing to educate, train and support people fully at the right time adds other significant risks, raising the level of resistance you can expect and also diminishing the returns on your project's investment.

Loss of Efficiency

Inexperienced project managers (and eternal optimists) will anticipate that the introduction of a new system, process or asset into an organisation will rapidly bring about the rise in efficiency that the business case predicted, as in Figure 10.1.

Figure 10.1: Predicted Efficiency Gains following Project Handover

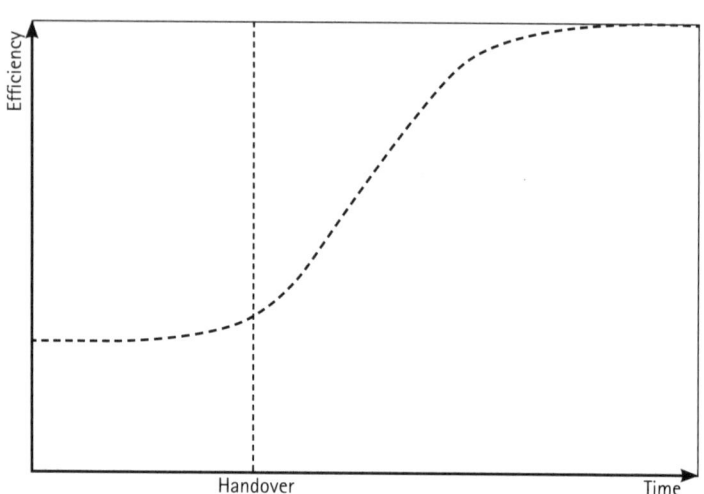

However, this is rarely the case. What we usually see is a curve like that illustrated in Figure 10.2.

Figure 10.2: Observed Efficiency Gains and Losses around Project Handover

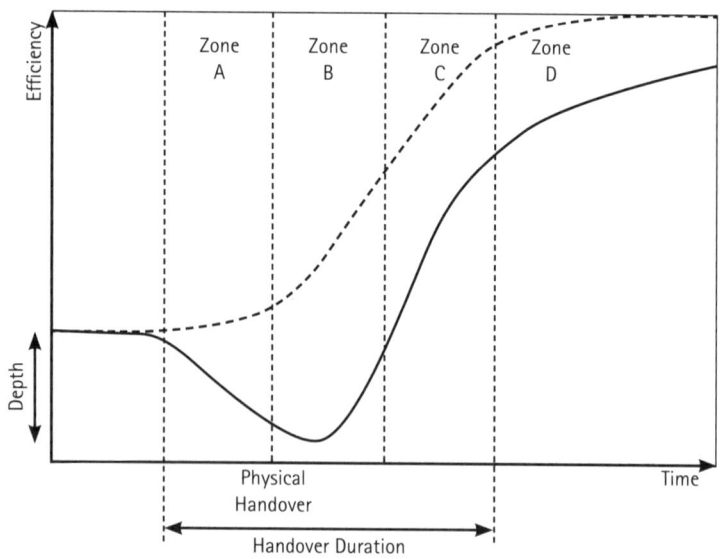

We can identify four time periods:

Zone A: Pre-Handover
Two factors combine to reduce operational efficiency ahead of handover:
1. Uncertainty, fear and confusion can affect morale and commitment and reduce operational efficiencies. This can start as early as when the project is first discussed, or as late as the lead-in to handover. Good communication is essential to minimise both the length of this period and also the depth of the dip in efficiency.
2. Ahead of handover, another loss of efficiency can occur as certain team members are diverted from operational work onto project activities. Who you schedule into project activities and how your operational colleagues manage the resultant vacuum will partly determine the breadth and depth of this dip.

Zone B: Post-Handover
In the period immediately after handover, people adapt to new ways of working. You can think of this period as the start of a "learning curve". Difficulties are at their peak, so efficiency is at a minimum. How you have prepared people, the level of support you give them, and the effectiveness of your communications in maintaining their motivation are the main levers for minimising both the depth and duration of this dip in efficiency.

Zone C: Recovery
As people start to understand their new way of working, skills, confidence and motivation will rise, with efficiency improving.

Zone D: Improvement
At some stage you will pass the break-even point and your new efficiency levels will exceed those of before the project. If your planning was good, you will be able to reach the anticipated efficiency level.

Incorporate the possibility of a temporary loss of efficiency into your risk planning, and look for ways to minimise both the duration and depth of the dip.

STAKEHOLDER ANALYSIS AND PLANNING

If your stakeholders pose a risk, you must identify, analyse and plan for that risk, and then deal with it. Figure 10.3 illustrates the stakeholder management process.

Figure 10.3: Stakeholder Management Process

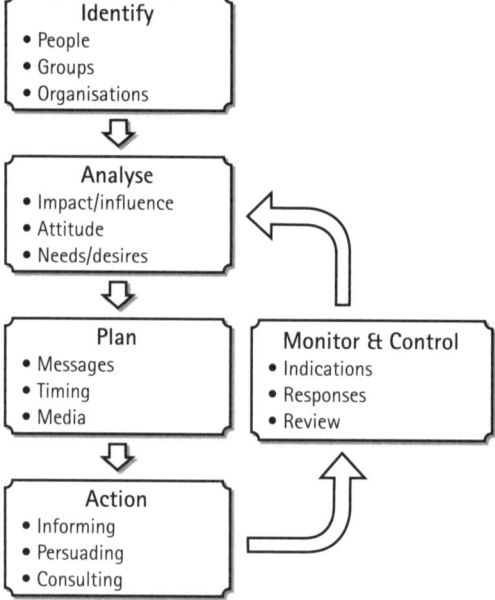

Identify

By now, this process should look familiar to you. Start by gathering your team together to identify the stakeholders. The more widely you cast your net, the better. Table 10.2 lists some typical project stakeholders.

Table 10.2: Examples of Project Stakeholders	
Internal to your organisation	Project sponsor Project user groups Project suppliers Senior management Line managers Staff Trades unions Shareholders, members or trustees Testers Training teams
External to your organisation	Local community Partners Customers Service users Suppliers Regulators, taxation authorities and other public authorities Competitors Investors, lenders and creditors Professional associations and trade bodies Pension holders and active pensioners Schools, colleges, employment services

Analyse

Once you have identified your stakeholders, analyse them to understand who they are; what their needs, interests and expectations are; their attitudes to your project; and how much influence they can exert over the success, or failure, of the project. What objectives do you need to establish in your relationship with each stakeholder? What does each stakeholder need (and want) to know?

Plan

Use your analysis as a basis to develop a plan for how you will manage your relationship with each stakeholder or stakeholder group to achieve your objectives.

Action, monitor and control

Once you have a plan, put it into action, and then continue to monitor its effectiveness. Analyse why it is or is not working and adjust your plan accordingly.

STAKEHOLDERS' ATTITUDES TO RISK

If you are following a structured approach to project risk management, then a major consideration (which we will examine in the next chapter) is your appetite for risk: that is, how much risk the sponsoring organisation is prepared to accept when it commits to the project.

Not all stakeholders will have the same attitude: some may believe you should incur less risk (risk aversion), while others would prefer you to be more adventurous (risk accepting). Where stakeholders have a different attitude to risk from the one that prevails within the project, this introduces another risk: that some stakeholders' actions can act as triggers for unwanted outcomes.

They may, for example, brief against the project or even against key project staff, taking them to task for perceived faulty decisions. They may trigger risks in trying to prove that they are right, or even act unilaterally by taking actions that lie outside of your project plan.

You must therefore consider the range of potential stakeholder attitudes to risk as part of your analysis. The following factors can influence how we perceive risk and hence our level of aversion or acceptance.

Table 10.3: Factors Affecting Stakeholders' Attitudes to Risk	
Perceptions	We act according to our perceptions of reality. Where your perceptions and those of your stakeholders differ, you can expect a different attitude to risk, too. Work hard to communicate a shared understanding of the project environment and status.
History	Experience colours not only our perception of things but, crucially, how we interpret them. So even if I read the project in the same way as you do, I may make a very different interpretation of what that means and consequently how to act. Much of politics is driven by this.
Public position	Making a "U-turn" is the right thing to do when facing in the wrong direction. Yet many people still find it difficult to admit an earlier fault. Stated public positions can therefore influence attitudes (more politics!). Ensure you do nothing to force people into stating a position publicly too early in the process.
Psychology	There are a host of psychological biases that influence our perception of risk. These are described in Chapter 12. Uncovering the sources of bias is the best way to challenge them.
Culture	Finally (even more politics here), much of our attitude to risk arises from cultural influences, whether they are national, regional, local, organisational, ethnic, social or anything else. Rather than assume an easy stereotype, however, talk to people to learn how their own individual influences have shaped their attitude to the risks of your project.

COMMUNICATION STRATEGY AND PLAN

The best approach to winning stakeholder support is through open, honest, two-way communication. As a project manager you will want to develop a communication strategy and plan. Communication is an ongoing process that will start with your project and only finish when it has been closed and fully evaluated. Good communication is essential, not just to manage risk, but also to manage the perception of risk.

Table 10.4 sets out the components of a communication strategy.

Table 10.4: Project Communication Strategy	
Stakeholder analysis	List of stakeholders and details of your analysis.
Communication objectives	Set out what you need to achieve and which risks communication will help to mitigate.
Available communication mechanisms	Be thorough in inventorying available media, and consider everything from simple low tech flip-chart posters and notes on noticeboards to websites, podcasts and videos. The lowest technology is the best of all: meet a person and talk with them.
Planning process and tools	How will you plan and what template will you use? Who has responsibility and what are the roles? What is the process for getting the plan approved? What is the timetable for planning and approval?
Monitoring and control	Who will monitor your plan, when will they do this and what will they be looking for?
Crisis communication	In Chapter 9 we briefly considered crisis management and the need to know who will communicate and how they will communicate in a crisis. Ensure you document this.

Table 10.5 illustrates the most important components of a communication plan for a single stakeholder or stakeholder group. Where your planning does not need to be as detailed, each stakeholder may represent one line on a plan covering a whole range of stakeholders.

Table 10.5: Stakeholder Communication Plan					
Stakeholder	[Name the stakeholder or stakeholder group]				
ID	Message	Timing	Method and medium	Feedback	Responsibilities

ID – As with all plans, it is a good idea to give each element a unique ID number. This will ideally flow directly from your project Work Breakdown Structure.

Message – Set out what different messages you need to communicate to the stakeholder. It is valuable to record the tone you want to take to help reduce the chances of miscommunication at a subconscious level. Do you want to enquire or require, tell or sell, teach or preach, consult or inform, request or command? When you have drafted your message, ask someone independent to assess the tone; is it the tone you had hoped for? If not, re-draft it. One of the trickiest things to communicate is your response to resistance. See *The Handling Resistance Pocketbook* listed in the Learn More section at the back of this book.

Timing – Set out when each communication should be made. With regular communications like progress reports, team meetings, or newsletters, set out the frequency, such as "monthly, on the first Tuesday".

Method and medium – Describe the best way to get each message across. To do this, consider:
- the nature of the message
- the culture of the stakeholders
- your intended "tone of voice" (formal or informal?).

Here is a chance to be creative in finding ways to get your message across effectively against a backdrop of the hundreds of other messages your stakeholders have to process each day.

Feedback – Once you have communicated, how will you know that your stakeholders have heard, understood and are going to act upon your message? Think about how you will test this out and gather feedback. This may be as simple as just listening to their response.

Responsibilities – Who is responsible for each communication? Who will provide any necessary information and who will collate it? Who drafts the message and who distributes it? Who will gather feedback, and who will analyse it?

CHAPTER 11
APPETITE FOR RISK

HOW MUCH ARE YOU PREPARED TO PUT AT RISK? The answer to this question is called your "appetite for risk". The amount can be expressed as a financial value, a delay, a potential disruption or even reputational risk. "Risk appetite" is the level of exposure to risk that you are prepared to tolerate.

Because risk considers both a potential threat and also a potential benefit, how does our definition apply to opportunities? To answer this, you must consider what level of investment you are prepared to make in the hope of securing the benefit, with the possibility of losing all. Calculating your appetite for risk recognises the need to make an investment to either reduce threat or maximise opportunity, so compares this investment cost with the value and likelihood of the improved outcome: lower threat or greater opportunity.

Two related terms are worth considering.
- *Risk capacity* is the level of exposure to risk that you are able to tolerate.
- *Risk exposure* is the value (materials, products, services and time) that you have placed at risk.

Risk Appetite as a Boundary

Perhaps the simplest way to think of risk appetite is as a boundary on our chart of likelihood against impact. Any risks to the upper right of that boundary (shaded) are beyond our appetite and are hence not tolerable.

Figure 11.1: Risk Appetite

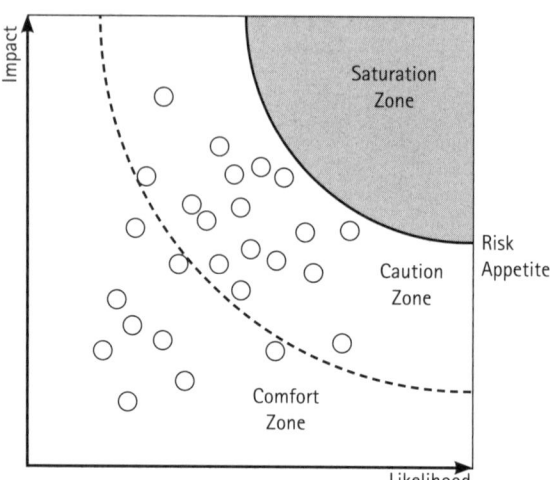

Normally, your risk capacity will exceed your risk appetite, offering a margin of comfort. In a highly risk-aggressive context, you might adopt a risk appetite position that exceeds your capacity to absorb the risk. This would only be appropriate where doing nothing involves significant risks.

You would also hope that normally your total risk exposure would lie within your caution zone. With an exposure in the saturation zone, you are exceeding your appetite for risk and will be constantly concerned or even fearful of the consequences. The risks will come to dominate your agenda. If your exposure lies in the comfort zone, however, you may be missing important opportunities. You may therefore choose to define a region of optimum risk exposure as well as your maximum appetite for risk.

ORGANISATIONAL APPETITE FOR RISK

Figure 11.1 illustrates concepts only. As you start to define your attitude to risk, you need to think about individual risks and the aggregate of all of your risks. What is most important is the decision-making process that underpins your appetite for risk. These are strategic level decisions that must be taken by people with the appropriate level of authority, and be properly communicated to the organisation and the project team.

The concept of risk appetite, capacity and exposure can be applied at every level of your organisation, from the corporate level down to your individual project. At a corporate level, it is common to consider a number of individual areas of risk that threaten the organisation and determine your capacity and appetite for risk in each area: for example, financial, regulatory, reputational and operational risk.

Some organisations – particularly those in the statutory sector, such as public authorities – will start with a presumption of risk aversion. It is not the role of publicly funded organisations to take risks with the services they provide. Typically it is the private sector that is risk tolerant, with entrepreneurial businesses having the greatest appetite for risk.

PROJECT APPETITE FOR RISK

A strategic view of project risk appetite begins by asking how much risk the organisation can tolerate from this project? The answer will depend on the project's goal and objectives. Where there is a huge benefit on offer from an innovative project that could radically enhance your competitive position, then you can justify a large appetite for risk. At the other extreme, a project to ensure regulatory compliance in a core part of your business cannot afford to expose your organisation to anything but the lowest threat levels.

A common method is to adopt a "portfolio approach" to project risk (which we will examine at the end of this chapter). As with any investment, a project can fail. By adopting a range of projects with differing risk and benefit profiles, organisations seek to achieve enough benefit from project successes to counter the failures of some high risk projects.

HOW RISKY IS YOUR PROJECT?

Chapter 9 began with the observation that risks accumulate on projects by multiplying one another rather than simply adding up. Calculating a total level of project risk is therefore a complex process and we considered tools like the Root Mean Squared (RMS) method and the Monte Carlo technique as helpful approaches in Chapter 5. Both of these, however, assume that risks are independent, which is rarely the case. The best approach is therefore to revert to something far simpler.

In Chapter 4, we described how you can use a project Risk Potential Review (RPR) to assess the overall level of project risk. The RPR can be used as a way of understanding what risks exist, and using a simple scoring system, of gauging the level of risk on a standardised basis.

This approach directs us towards the factors that tend to make a project risky.

Table 11.1: Typical Factors Leading to a High Risk Project

Strategic factors
- Weak link between project and organisational strategy
- Low levels of ownership at senior levels, and poor sponsorship
- Unclear success criteria (goal and objectives poorly defined; scope under-defined or shifting)
- Unrealistic expectations

Capability factors
- Unskilled project leadership (project manager, project sponsor)
- Insufficient skills and experience among project team
- Insufficient resources allocated (or unrealistic expectations)
- Project disciplines unfamiliar at the required scale

Process factors
- Complex and shifting stakeholder attitudes
- Poor communication between the project team and partner organisations
- Under-tested or poorly understood technology
- Inadequate governance or quality assurance processes

Organisational factors
- Undeveloped or inappropriate procurement practices
- Low morale
- Over-concentration of price as the measure of value
- Resistance to change

PERSONAL APPETITE FOR RISK

As individuals, we each have a different appetite for risk based on our personality and personal preferences, which can manifest in anything from a severe aversion, to tolerance, resilience and finally an enthusiasm for risk. To start to understand this better, it is wise to separate out the two chief aspects of risk: uncertainty and consequences.

Some people like uncertainty and enjoy taking new opportunities as they arise, readily casting aside any existing plans. They tend to be spontaneous, playful and dislike making decisions, which they see as closing down their options. Others cleave to their plans and feel uncomfortable when asked to change them at short notice. They crave certainty.

Adventurers find the possibility of calamity stimulating. It gives them a buzz of adrenalin that makes them feel more alive. Others like the comfort of knowing that nothing bad can happen to them.

Personality Types

When we put these two attitudes together, we can identify four personality types.

Figure 11.2: Personality driven by Attitudes to Uncertainty and Consequences

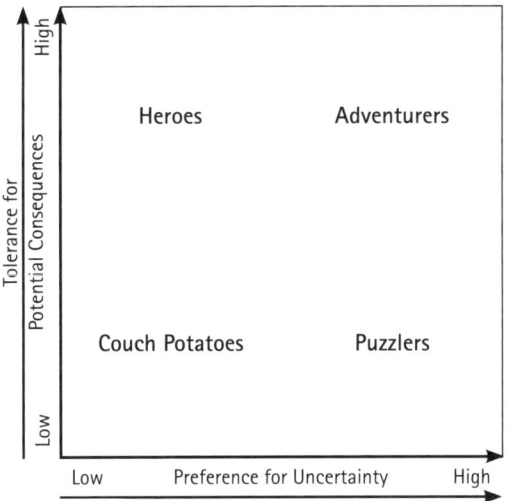

In Figure 11.2, adventurers like high risk and uncertain situations. But they can make poor risk managers, who must also be adept at dealing with and reducing the level of risk. Figure 11.3 combines appetite for risk with confidence in problem solving.

Figure 11.3: Risk Managers in Context

Personality Clash

Projects can run into problems when key people have conflicting attitudes to risk, or the attitudes of project leaders do not match the needs of the project. A project with a low tolerance for risk and a "hero" workstream leader can soon find the workstream is out of control. A "comfort seeker" project manager will not be comfortable leading a high-risk project.

The best solution is to appoint a project manager who has a "risk manager" profile of being comfortable in an unpredictable and threatening environment, who is also a confident problem solver. If this person can also harness the talents of "thrill seekers" and "challenge seekers" in doing the risky activities and designing solutions respectively, you have the basis of a dream team.

WHICH PROJECTS TO DO?

The discipline of project management has evolved rapidly over the last 30 years. To project management has been added *programme management* – the coordination of interacting, inter-dependent or related projects as a whole, as well as *portfolio management* – the processes that co-ordinate the selection, delivery and evaluation of programmes and projects. Together, you may hear of them as *P3M* – portfolio, programme and project management.

The concept of project and programme portfolios goes back to the investment markets of the 1940s and 1950s. In 1952, Harry Markowitz published a landmark academic paper that showed how investors could spread their risk by holding a range of different investments. Whilst some will fail, others would prosper. Statistics showed that, in the absence of major systemic effects (like a global economic crisis), such a portfolio of investments performed well – although not spectacularly. In statistical jargon, this is known as "regression to the mean". The performance of a suitably mixed basket of investments will mirror the average performance of all possible investments. It takes the risk out of choosing which investments to hold. (It does not, however, remove the risk of choosing to invest: you may not be putting all of your eggs in one basket, but you are relying on eggs for your dinner.)

Portfolio management in the context of projects and programmes takes the same approach. Since projects and programmes are inherently risky, we can limit our risk by carrying out a carefully chosen portfolio of projects and programmes. Some will do spectacularly well and will balance those that fail.

Organisations should no longer select a single future/goal and choose only projects that will confidently take them in that direction. Now, we see organisations conducting scenario analysis (see Chapter 9) and commissioning a range of projects that can accommodate a number of possible futures. Some of these will need to be cancelled as events modify the futures they are predicated on. Others will fail, and others will succeed. As long as the successes outweigh the failure, the portfolio approach is a success.

In the UK, the Office for Government Commerce (OGC), who own and maintain the formal PRINCE2 project management methodology (which is mandatory for all UK public bodies) are in the process, as this book is being written, of finalising their own Portfolio Management Guide.

Threat and Benefit Analysis

There are many tools available to help you build a balanced project portfolio, most of which are outside the scope of this book. One, however, will help you understand potential projects in terms of risk, illustrated in Figure 11.4.

Figure 11.4: Threat and Benefit Analysis for Potential Projects

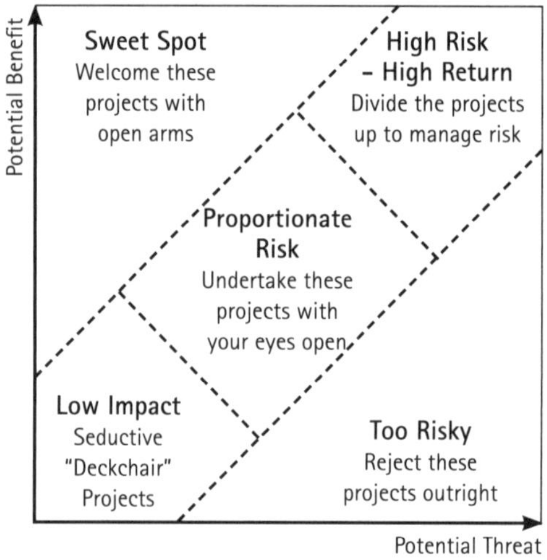

```
Potential Benefit ↑
                    Sweet Spot              High Risk
                    Welcome these           - High Return
                    projects with           Divide the projects
                    open arms               up to manage risk

                          Proportionate
                              Risk
                          Undertake these
                          projects with
                          your eyes open

                    Low Impact
                    Seductive               Too Risky
                    "Deckchair"             Reject these
                    Projects                projects outright
                                                    → Potential Threat
```

In this approach, you will plot your risks on a chart showing potential benefit against potential threat. The chart is divided into five areas, with the position of the two long diagonal boundaries representing your appetite for risk. Moving these boundaries downwards and to the right represents a greater appetite for risk.

Sweet Spot – Projects that offer high potential benefits with little or no threat require little further analysis once their position on the chart is confirmed. All that remains is to ensure that you have sufficient resources to manifest the benefits whilst keeping the threats contained.

Too Risky – Likewise, once you have set the boundary of your risk appetite, any project that offers too little benefit for the threat incurred must be rejected.

Proportionate Risk – Projects in the middle diagonal band all have a proportionate balance of risk and return. In the middle of this region, if you take on the project with your eyes open, the threats are manageable and you can achieve valuable benefits for your client.

Low Impact – At the bottom left of the proportionate band are low-risk, low-return projects. These are seductive because they can be completed easily. However, if you take on too many of these, you will dissipate a lot of resources and energy on what will ultimately have little real benefit. These projects give the illusion of progress but have no significant value. They are like moving the deckchairs around on the Titanic.

High Risk, High Return – At the top righthand end of the band are big projects with a lot of risk. Whilst the ultimate pay-off may be big, they are like the gamble of carrying all of your eggs in one basket. The portfolio approach would suggest you divide these projects up into smaller, less risky elements that can collectively have a similar level of benefit, but threat levels that are easier to manage.

CHAPTER 12
THE PSYCHOLOGY OF RISK

PEOPLE ARE IRRATIONAL. We often say it with a sense of irony when things go wrong, but economists and social psychologists who have been studying our behaviour when we make decisions have come to a worrying conclusion. Irrationality is not an aberrant behaviour: it is the norm.

Nothing illustrates this better than the simple experiment that economist Richard Thaler carried out at the start of his career. He asked people two questions that, rationally, should have the same answer:
1. How much would you be willing to pay to eliminate a 1:1000 chance of immediate death?
2. How much would you need to be paid to accept a 1:1000 chance of immediate death?

Both questions should logically yield the value of a life, by multiplying the answer by one thousand. However, Thaler got very different answers; typically hundreds of dollars for the first and tens of thousands for the second.

Psychological Bias

This is an example of a psychological bias. In this case, we are biased to protect what we already feel we own. In the former case, it is our money, and in the latter case, it is our life. We therefore put a greater value on what we already own. Thaler, with colleagues Daniel Kahneman and Jack L. Knetsch, showed the absurdity even more clearly by giving some students (the "sellers") a mug, and asking how much they would sell it for, and by asking others (the "buyers") how much they would buy the mug for. The sellers valued the mug they owned at $7.12; the buyers valued them at $2.87. This bias is known as the *endowment effect*, or *loss aversion*.

Heuristics

Along with Thaler, the two other leading researchers in this area are Daniel Kahneman and Amos Tversky (who died in 1996). They focused on the simple rules that we deploy, unconsciously, to make decisions. These unwritten rules are often unknown to us and are called heuristics. Heuristics lead to more bias.

This chapter is about the hard-wired heuristics that affect our estimating process and our evaluation of risk, the cultural effects on our perceptions of risk and the way we make group decisions.

INDIVIDUAL BIASES
The Gambler's Run Trap

Imagine I flip a coin and get heads... three times in a row. You know that there is a 50:50 chance of getting tails, so you cannot help but think that a throw of tails is "due". Subconsciously, we feel that a run of luck must change. Yet, if the coin is honest, the next toss still has a 50:50 chance of coming up heads; and it always will do, even after a run of 6, 60 or 600 throws. The belief that because a random event has not happened yet, it must be about to happen – or if it's been happening a lot, it must be due to stop – is a fallacy.

The Anchoring Bias

This predisposes us to make inferences based on the first information we get – even if that information has little or no relevance. If someone in a group states a preference, a belief, or a position, then our analysis tends to take that as a starting point. If it is the wrong starting point, we can end up in the wrong place. This is also known as the *primacy trap*.

Pattern Making

Human beings are pattern-forming creatures, so when we see something that appears to fit a familiar or typical pattern, we tend to believe that the pattern is at work, rather than coincidence. We will therefore over-estimate the likelihood of risks that seem familiar or which flow from an obvious logical pattern. Random and unfamiliar events seem less likely than they really are. This is also known as the *representativeness bias*.

The Availability Bias

Information that is readily to hand figures more highly in our perception of risk than other information that is not so fresh in our minds. For example, a recent incident at a nuclear power plant seems more salient than the many hundreds of unreported accidents and fatalities in the coal mining industry. Recent events bias our perception of risk, because they are more available to our intuition than alternative examples. This is also known as the *recency trap*.

Dread

Another bias arises from an unconscious mixing of likelihood and impact. As we saw in Chapter 5, the worse the outcome, the greater our estimation of the likelihood of an event happening. We rate higher impact events as more likely to occur than they really are. This, too, affects our perceptions of nuclear risk. Fear of nuclear accidents blinds us to the greater injury and fatality risks of coal mining, not just because of our lesser familiarity with the risks inherent in the coal industry (see the *availability bias*, above) but also because of our fear of the scale of a possible accident. This is also called the *affect bias*, because it is how the perceived risk affects us that influences our estimation.

The Control Bias

We also saw in Chapter 5 how our perception that bad things are less likely to occur when we are in control distorts our perception of risk when somebody else is. We over-estimate the risk, even when someone highly skilled is in control.

Contamination

Another distortion comes when we consider the context of a risk. We also consider a bad outcome is more likely when it is associated with something we consider to be, in itself, bad. So, we feel more likely to catch a dreaded disease in an unfamiliar country, while industrial accidents seem more likely in a "bad" industry. What is important is not an objective assessment of the context (you can decide for yourself which countries or industries feel bad to you). What matters in influencing your perception of likelihood is your subjective assessment of the context.

The "Confirming Evidence" Trap

One of the nastiest biases we have is the confirming evidence bias, which leads our brains to spot evidence that supports what we already believe we *know* to be true, whilst failing to notice any evidence that doesn't support our preconceived notions. Not only has this accounted for academics ignoring experimental data that could lead to a revolution in our understanding, it is the source of many of our prejudices. In management theory, it is known as the "horns and halo" effect. If I think you are a poor performer, I will spot all of your shortcomings and barely credit your triumphs. If I think you are a star, I can easily overlook your failings. In neither case am I objective or fair.

In a project environment, if our experience leads us to one conclusion, we can easily be blind to evidence that we are wrong. This is why you must always start preparing a formal report by examining all of the data with a colleague, before summarising its implications and drawing conclusions. If, instead, you start by writing your assessment of the situation and draw data to support it, you are far more likely to miss the important facts that tell a different story.

CULTURAL THEORY OF RISK

In 1982, Mary Douglas (a British anthropologist) and Aaron Wildavsky (an American political scientist) wrote *Risk and Culture: An Essay on the Selection of Technical and Environmental Dangers*, in which they set out their "cultural theory of risk".

Different societies and different cultures have their own ways of interpreting events and situations, which leads to very different perceptions of risk. Douglas had categorised societies by comparing levels of hierarchy versus equality, and according to the level of collective control versus self-sufficiency. In *Risk and Culture*, the authors suggest that these different ways of life lead to different attitudes to risk. They focused on the then emerging awareness of environmental risks. Douglas identified four broad cultural categories and characterised them thus:

1. **Fatalistic** – "What will happen, will happen, so I have little concern for risk."
2. **Egalitarian** – "We have a stewardship role, and therefore personal responsibility makes me fearful of risk."
3. **Individualistic** – "Nothing must over-ride my personal rights, so I ignore risks."
4. **Hierarchical** – "The structures of society are paramount, so I see risks as subordinate to society."

There is little empirical research behind these cultural groupings or their attitudes to risk, but the wider anthropological point must surely be valid: our culture and upbringing conditions the way we see the world and therefore how we are pre-disposed to identify and evaluate risk.

GROUP THINK AND RISKY SHIFT
Group Think

In the 1970s, the social psychologist Irving Janis examined how groups make decisions. He found that a group's dynamic often inhibits exploration of alternatives. People find disagreement uncomfortable, so the group seeks consensus before it has reached a satisfactory conclusion. As the group approaches consensus, dissenting voices are rejected or, indeed, are often self-censored. Janis wrote: "Concurrence-seeking becomes so dominant in a cohesive group that it tends to over-ride realistic appraisal of alternative courses of action."

When we fall prey to Group Think, decisions tend to be based on "what we all know" – that is, members are inhibited from challenging the consensus and relevant information, ideas and challenges are not fully explored. Janis described Group Think as occurring "When the member's strivings for unanimity override their motivation to realistically appraise alternative courses of action."

Risky Shift

As a result of Group Think, the group tends to a higher collective confidence in a decision than individuals have in the same decision made separately. Therefore, with dissent discouraged, groups tend to endorse higher risk decisions than individuals would. Psychologists refer to this as "risky shift".

People with more extreme positions are more likely than others to develop clear arguments and are also most likely to voice them. We saw above the effects of the "anchoring trap": the order in which people speak can affect the course of a discussion. Comments early in a debate are more influential in forming opinions and also create the framework for the discussion. Where Group Think starts to endorse a decision at one extreme, members of the group may be emboldened to put forward still more extreme points of view.

Risky shift is the difference between the average risk taken by individuals and the risk taken by the group. This can generate either a risky shift towards a higher risk position or, equally, a cautious shift towards a more risk-averse stance.

Doing Away with Group Think

In his powerful book, *The Wisdom of Crowds*, James James Surowiecki writes: "In unstructured, free flowing discussions, the information that tends to be talked about the most is, paradoxically, the information that everyone already knows."

Therefore, to prevent Group Think, you must ensure that new information can be introduced, dissenting voices can be heard and criticisms can be made.

Appoint a devil's advocate – The first idea is to ask one member of the team to play the role of "devil's advocate" and seek to oppose any consensus with contrary evidence, different logic, fresh interpretations or a new perspective. In their book, *The Corporate Fool*, David Firth and Alan Leigh identify different ways we can shake up the soft thinking and status quo of organisations by borrowing from the different roles of the medieval ruler's fool. The "contrarian" challenges norms and the "truth-seeker" tells difficult truths. This is just the cure for Group Think.

Encourage everyone to be a critical evaluator – There is no reason why we should not all adopt the devil's advocate role. Edward de Bono's "Six Thinking Hats" approach to critical and creative thinking suggests that two hats – the White Hat and the Black Hat – encourage us to assess the evidence logically and with all of the available data (White Hat) and to challenge, criticise and evaluate all that has been proposed (Black Hat). As a project manager, encourage your team members to all put on their White Hats and Black Hats from time to time, to avoid sliding into Group Think.

Do not let the leader state a preference up front – There are many types of "leader" in a discussion: the chair or facilitator, the expert, the boss. All of these individuals can have a disproportionate impact on the group's thinking, arising from the expert or hierarchical status they possess. To help avoid group members being seduced by the leader's point of view, ask them to hold it back until after the main discussion. This has a large extra advantage: when we state our position, it becomes harder to change it and often this is even more the case when we see ourselves as leaders or experts – we fear losing face. By encouraging the leaders and experts to not state their position, you make it easier for them to evaluate the arguments they hear and therefore re-evaluate their own thinking.

Set up independent groups – If a group is susceptible to Group Think, it will fight hard to have its point of view adopted. By splitting it into two or more independent sub-groups, you encourage each to think for itself. Even if the new groupings fall prey to Group Think and risky shift, they are unlikely to end up at the same position. So bring them back together to share their thinking in plenary. This way you will hear a range of arguments.

Invite new people into the group – When you bring new people into a group, you do more than just introduce fresh ideas. With no group allegiance, they will not feel the same pressure to conform. And, as an outsider, they will be unlikely to share the group's acquired biases and prejudices. They will need to ask questions to understand arguments and will not settle for easy and weak answers. Most of all, they bring diversity of ideas, thinking styles and knowledge.

Gather anonymous feedback – When we contribute anonymously to an argument, we are far more comfortable and likely to say what we really think. How can you use suggestion boxes, an online forum or an independent intermediary to encourage honest feedback and genuine contributions? This is, of course, the basis of the Delphi technique, described in Chapter 4.

Wisdom of Crowds and Conditions for Effective Group Decisions

James Surowiecki's book, *The Wisdom of Crowds*, gives many examples of when a team can be wiser than individuals ... and also of when groups make disastrous decisions. He identifies three criteria for a team to act effectively:

- **Independence**

  Each group member must be able to think independently, be allowed to speak their own mind and be listened to attentively.

- **Diversity**

  A range of perspectives are important. The single biggest influence on team success is the diversity of opinion, ways of thinking, experiences, expertise and viewpoints. Surowiecki found that "the presence of a minority viewpoint, all by itself, makes a group's decisions more nuanced and its decision-making process more rigorous".

- **Decentralisation**

  Everyone involved in the decision-making process must have independent access to all available data, so that they are free to evaluate it and interpret it as they choose.

CHAPTER 13
RISK CULTURE

THIS FINAL CHAPTER LOOKS at the organisational culture that needs to surround your project: the decision making, oversight and policy infrastructure, and the processes and procedures that support these things.

A strong organisational risk management culture will give you the potential to incorporate organisational learning from previous projects into your plan. We will focus on how you can identify lessons from your own project to feed back in to it. If you do not enjoy a robust organisational infrastructure that will store and disseminate your learning effectively, then the principal reason for doing this is for the benefit of the team of people working together on your project. When you carry out a "lessons learned review" effectively, everyone present will be wiser for their next project; this is more than enough reason on its own for doing it.

There are real benefits in maintaining a strong organisational risk management culture.

Table 13.1: Typical Benefits of a Strong Risk Management Culture
Systems and procedures • Standard templates and tools • Documentation to guide action • Training and consistency • Optimised processes and efficiency <div align="right">*more >>>*</div>

Attitudes and values
- Understanding and appreciation of uncertainty
- Risk awareness and prudent behaviours
- Shared language and methodologies provide consistent approaches
- Risk treated as a business issue

Records and history
- Knowledge base to support organisational learning
- An understanding of the factors in past successes and failures
- Benchmarks and metrics
- Data for estimating budgets, schedules and risk likelihood

Probity and control
- Oversight gives the ability to challenge and affect what is done
- Accountable and transparent decision-making process
- Evidence-based policy, strategy and plan development
- Conscious choice of risk profile at all levels

BUILDING A STRONG RISK MANAGEMENT CULTURE

The basic foundations for a risk-aware, risk-responsible culture are strong processes with a supporting infrastructure, and people to effectively implement it. Your people must have both the commitment and the capability to get it right.

Nothing, however, is more important than the tone set by the organisation's leaders. This is not just senior management, but the people who oversee them: ministers and elected members in the public sector, trustees in the charitable sector and non-executive directors in the private sector. No amount of documented processes and written best practices, nor tools and templates will succeed where people at the top do not conspicuously value the principle of good risk management.

If leaders are prepared to lead on this matter, and provide the funding and resources that are required, Table 13.2 sets out the elements of a strong risk management culture that you should focus on creating.

Table 13.2: Elements of a Strong Organisational Risk Culture

Leadership	Leadership needs to be conspicuous and accountable at executive level, and mirrored by firm commitment and oversight at non-executive level.
Policies	Develop a set of guiding policies that reflect the nature of your organisation and its business and the nature of the risks you face. These should also identify responsibilities at the highest levels and, in particular, who at top level will sponsor the introduction and maintenance of risk management. Policy should also identify how risk is monitored at board level.
Processes	Develop clear, easy to use and effective processes that match the needs of your organisation. Better a concise process that is well-used than a comprehensive one that is soon abandoned or used only sporadically. Once designed, periodically review and develop your processes. They need to be clearly documented and widely disseminated. Integrate your processes with: • Supporting infrastructure like tools, templates, contract forms and technology • Reporting processes and how you communicate with your organisation and stakeholders • Systems for organisational learning and knowledge management, if you have them • Escalation procedures • Welcoming and induction programme for new recruits • Programme and project management processes
Tools	Build a set of tools that are adapted to your organisation's needs. The most fundamental will be a risk register, but you will find many more in this book and beyond, all the way up to complex and costly enterprise-scale software products.
Capability	Set up a programme to create a cadre of trained and capable people who share a common understanding, language and toolset. After training, create opportunities to use their new knowledge and develop their skills, judgement and awareness. Make suitable reference material readily available and encourage the sharing of experiences and learning.
Incentives	Provide appropriate incentives (and, indeed compulsions) to ensure that people comply intelligently with processes and procedures that have been developed. This is not about compelling strict, unthinking adherence, but about ensuring that people know what is expected of them and that this expectation is a part of their terms and conditions of employment. The old saying, "what gets measured gets managed", is true here. If you do not monitor and gather data on risk management activities, then there will be little incentive for people to comply. Likewise, if senior management and the governance bodies of your organisation do not review what this data is telling them and act on what they learn, then poor performance will be tolerated.
Review	Periodic critical review is essential if you want to maintain and grow a strong risk management culture. Encourage external review as well as internal assessments and take opportunities to learn from other organisations – both similar and very different. You may find that direct comparisons (or "benchmarking") among comparable organisations will give all participants valuable insights.
Embedding	All of the above must be embedded seamlessly into other organisational processes and procedures, so that risk management does not stand alone within your organisation, but rather feels like an organic part of everything that you do.

Steps in Creating a Strong Risk Culture

Whilst this is in no way a comprehensive process for creating a strong risk culture, the following steps set out some of the key elements that any organisation should pursue.

Table 13.3: Steps in Creating a Strong Organisational Risk Culture	
Sponsorship	i. The process must start with someone at a very senior level taking ownership. ii. They must win support and commitment across the top of the organisation among executive and non-executive leaders. iii. This commitment must be conspicuous to all and backed up by funding and resources.
Communication	i. Start communicating the imperative and intent early on. ii. Identify and analyse stakeholders and build a thorough communications plan. iii. Create a reporting process to ensure your sponsor and senior team can monitor and guide progress.
Team	i. Find people with the right breadth of skills and experience to work on the project. ii. Brief your team to ensure a common understanding; if necessary, provide training or other development opportunities. iii. Research your work through reading and speaking with colleagues. Make contact with other organisations and arrange site visits.
Basics	i. Create a process with basic supporting tools. ii. Make them effective – but do not aim for them to be perfect. iii. Get the process implemented on a pilot basis.
Quick wins	i. Look for opportunities to demonstrate the value of what you are doing. ii. Communicate successes widely. iii. Engage champions from among the people who have seen success, to spread the word.
Learning and development	i. Evaluate pilot applications and discover what works and what does not. ii. Develop the processes and tools and supplement with more tools. iii. Develop briefing and training materials.
Roll-out	i. Create a training programme and schedule staff to attend modules designed for their work. ii. Maintain your communication process relentlessly. iii. Set up mechanisms to support practitioners who are using your new processes and tools.
Embedding and reviewing	i. Assess progress periodically. ii. Scan your business, political and competitive environment for changes that should inform regular reviews of your processes, tools and decision criteria. iii. Consolidate performance and reward successes.

A Risk Management Maturity Model

One of the big progressions in project management and its related disciplines over the last 20 years has been the development of *maturity models*. These consist of a set of criteria that allow an organisation to gauge its effectiveness in institutionalising good practices. The approach has been applied to project management, programme management, management of change and to risk management.

There are a number of proprietary risk management maturity models with between 4-6 levels and between 5-12 criteria to assess the levels. Most have their roots in a particular industry sector and culture, so for example, the UK Government's Management of Risk methodology has a 5-level model with 12 criteria, and the US Risk and Insurance Management Society has a model with 5 levels and 7 criteria.

Most track back to the Capability Maturity Model that was developed by the Carnegie Mellon University Software Engineering Institute (SEI), first described in the book *Managing the Software Process* by Watts Humphrey, published in 1989. They retain its original 5 levels and much of its terminology. Table 13.4 sets out some basic levels using widely applied terms. It should not be read as conforming to any of the proprietary published models.

Table 13.4: Risk Management Maturity Levels	
Level 1 *Ad Hoc*	No formal processes, nor recognition of the need for one. Any good work is done independently by individuals. Another term sometimes use for this level is "naïve".
Level 2 *Novice*	Awareness of need for systematic approach. Stated requirements for risk management with little more than generic guidance and no substantial training available. Tools are "home-made".
Level 3 *Repeatable*	First documentation of policies and procedures is produced, with responsibilities allocated and some training available. People are aware of shortcomings and gaps. Simple tools are available.
Level 4 *Managed*	Clear metrics established to guide implementation and decision making. Formal procedures are followed and individual levels of expertise are recognised, with incremental training and development available. Sophisticated tools are available.
Level 5 *Embedded*	Risk management is embedded in all organisational processes and is a part of the day-to-day culture. Knowledge, skills and techniques are constantly reviewed, with the organisation seen as a source of excellence and its senior practitioners regarded as leading experts.

IDENTIFYING AND LEARNING LESSONS

"Those who cannot remember the past are condemned to repeat it," wrote philosopher George Santayana. Frequently, we come across projects repeating the mistakes made by earlier projects. It is important not just to identify the lessons of a completed project, but to learn from them too!

There are two principal reasons to conduct a post-project, lessons-learned review: for the benefit of the organisation, and for the benefit of the people involved in the project. Firstly, decide which is the more important objective, because each will imply different questions and possibly a different process. If you choose to pursue both, then it can help if you hold the review meeting in two parts.

For the Benefit of the Organisation

Estimates – of time, budget, resource utilisation and the outcomes of predicted risks – are one of the most important areas to examine for the benefit of the organisation. If your primary purpose is to reflect on how well the project went, then ask the following questions:

- What were our intended results – what did we plan to do?
  What were our actual results – what really happened?
- What caused our results?
  Why did it happen that way?
- What risks did we anticipate?
  What risks materialised?
- What will we sustain and what will we improve?
  What will we do next time as a result of our learning?

However, if you want to focus on learning lessons, you will want a more reflective process. Three good questions to ask are:

- What ideas, contributions or events made the most difference to the project?
- What were the most surprising events and outcomes?
- What would be your priorities on day one of a similar project?

Risk Culture 157

Some organisations keep a lessons learned register. An example is shown in Table 13.5.

Table 13.5: Lessons Learned Register						
Unique ID	Project concerned	Date	Lesson learned	Author	Recommendations or follow-up actions	Responsibility

As with our risk registers, the ID and date help create an audit trail, while the need for a name of someone responsible for any follow-up actions or recommendations should be evident. A great way to describe the lesson learned is to divide it into cause and effect: "this is what happened, and this is why". With this approach you are likely to identify multiple recommendations and actions to be taken.

For the Benefit of the People Involved in the Project

What your people most need is to consolidate the skills they have used and turn them into positive assets. The biggest mistake in any review is to only focus on what went wrong. If you are familiar with the framework of Appreciative Inquiry, this is a good way to conduct your review.

In brief, Appreciative Inquiry is a process of asking questions that uncover positive potential by finding and celebrating the best of what is, and imagining what might be. In this approach, the value of a lessons learned review is not in the neat document you produce at the end, but in the quality of the stories, folklore and rules of thumb that your project generates.

Style

Whichever focus you put on your review, it is not so much what you do as how you do it. Aim to create a no-blame, no finger-pointing environment in which everyone has a say, is confident to speak out, and is willing to learn by discussing what happened in an objective manner. This is more important than any particular methodology or template. A skilled facilitator will do this by helping the group establish ground rules that they are comfortable with. Also, the facilitator can set an example with their own approach, including such basics as respectful behaviours, choice of language and tone of voice.

Agenda

Table 13.6 offers you a sample agenda for a post-project risk review. This is likely to form a part of your wider project review.

Table 13.6: Post-Project Risk Review	
Introductions	You won't need ice-breakers, but ensure everybody in the workshop is introduced.
COMB	An excellent way to start any meeting is to frame the COMB: *Context* — Why you called the meeting *Objectives* — What you want the meeting to achieve *Map* — The agenda you propose to follow *Benefits* — What participants will get from contributing
Risk register	Review the risk register, looking particularly at: • Risks that materialised – how well did the management plans work? • Risks that did not materialise – with the benefit of hindsight, how sound were assumptions over likelihood? • Numbers of risks identified, managed to closure and incurred.
Unforeseen events	What risks did you fail to foresee, and what process could have helped identify them in advance? What project assumptions were faulty?
Change log	What can the change log teach you about your risk management? What were the numbers of scope changes and the level of substandard deliverables that had to be reworked?
Plan	What can your planned and actual schedule, and your budget and actual costs teach you about your planning assumptions and risk management? Where did the project slip and catch up against schedule?
Risk management processes	How well did your risk management process work? What would you add, enhance, abandon or keep next time?
Next steps review	End your workshop with a summary of what the team has agreed, what actions each person has committed to, and the next steps for you and for the team. These are likely to include documenting the meeting with contributions to any lessons learned and project closure documents. The last thing you should do is to thank your colleagues for their contributions.

AN OUTSIDE PERSPECTIVE

The final word in this chapter is about the value of objectivity. No matter how well you run your project and regardless of how strong the risk management culture is within your organisation, there is always a role for an external facilitator to examine project risk. The external perspective brings two principal benefits.

- The first benefit is in driving the process by highlighting the accountabilities and responsibilities you have established and holding people fully to account.
- The second is in driving objectivity and realism in the assessment. An external facilitator can act as a critical friend in raising awareness and challenging thinking.

Your external facilitator can come from within your organisation or be independent, but they must bring true objectivity to the project. You can use such a person to audit your risk management or to facilitate discussions. For large and high-risk projects, this is a valuable addition to the overall project risk management process.

CONCLUSION

WE SWIM IN AN OCEAN OF RISK, and when we take on a project, with its various complexities, novelty, time constraints and requirement to coordinate multiple lines of activity to produce something to a specification, we step straight into the deepest part.

Does that mean that we should fear risk, or even do nothing? An old proverb says that a tortoise can only move forward when it sticks its head out from under its shell; and so it is for us. We must move forward confidently with a determination to acknowledge the risks that we face and manage them actively. Shift happens! What you can do is use the tools, the ideas and – most of all – the processes in this book to understand what could happen and prepare for it. Don't worry about shift: do something about it.

> *Worry does not empty tomorrow of its sorrow. It empties today of its strength!*
>
> Corrie ten Boom

APPENDIX A: LIST OF COMMON PROJECT RISKS

WHAT COULD POSSIBLY GO WRONG?

The following is not intended to be a complete answer to that question – you will need to assemble a diverse team and work this one through for yourself. However, the list below sets out many of the common and generic risks that can threaten a project. They are arranged according to the risk categories in Table 4.6 (on page 51).

Marketplace risks
- Political change
- Change in legislation/regulation
- Macro-economic changes
- Demand untested
- Demand drops/increases
- Vendor/supplies unavailable
- Supplier stops trading
- Sub-contractor failure
- Mergers/acquisitions
- Response to commercial tenders
- Breakdown of commercial relationship
- Disputes and claims

Technical risks
- Unrealistic functionality expectations
- Unrealistic quality expectations
- Complexity
- Novelty
- Scope creep
- Security
- Interface management
- Configuration management
- Reliability
- Maintenance

People risks
- Loss of a key person
- Stakeholder resistance
- Key people not involved
- Change of sponsorship
- Insufficient resources
- Insufficient capabilities
- Availability of experts
- Cultural clashes
- Strike
- Absences
- Illness
- Accidents
- Criminal acts
- Negligence
- Poor workmanship
- Transport failure
- Public perception
- Pressure groups and NGOs

Appendix A: List of Common Project Risks

Process risks
- Performance measures not set
- Performance measures inappropriate
- Inadequate or unreliable base data
- Loss of key data
- Organisational structure mismatched
- Poor governance
- Inadequate oversight
- Weak decision processes
- Poor estimating
- Team miscommunications
- Maintenance failure
- Stock control

Property risks
- Damp/rot/mould
- Pests
- Hazardous materials
- Contamination
- Waste disposal
- Theft
- Equipment failure
- Power failure
- Security risks
- Planning constraints
- Tree preservation orders (TPOs)
- Rights of way disputes
- Access disputes
- Boundary disputes
- Ownership disputes
- Statutory undertaker (gas, electric, water, waste) lead times

Financial risks
- Loss of funding
- Inadequate budget
- Budget over-runs
- Cash flow
- Change of ownership of business
- Contract defaults
- Price variances
- Inflation
- Taxation
- Interest rates
- Exchange rates
- Bond yields
- Market appetite
- Availability of credit
- Fraud

Natural and social risks
- Weather – rain, snow, cold, heat, wind
- Earthquake
- Flood
- Landslip
- Civil unrest
- General strikes
- Terrorism
- War
- Epidemic
- Pestilence
- Famine

APPENDIX B: GLOSSARY

Acceptance	A strategy of being prepared to tolerate a risk, should it manifest, and therefore not making any advance plans to mitigate it.
Agile project management	A project management methodology (most often used for software projects) where progress is made in short bursts of activity, followed by review and planning for the next burst. It is designed to speed up development and better accommodate frequent and late changes in specification, scope or technology solution.
Appreciative Inquiry (AI)	Asking questions to access an organisation's full potential, by valuing the best of what is available, rather than deprecating the worst.
Assurance	Process of independent review of a project to ensure it follows sound procedures and good governance, and is delivering to its objectives.
Benefit	An improvement or advantage gained by the organisation as a result of the project. Benefits can be financial or non-financial in nature. They can be quantifiable or non-quantifiable, although some organisations choose to ignore non-quantifiable benefits in establishing a business case. Some exclude all non-financial benefits.
Business case	An analysis of the benefits and costs of making a change to a project's working method.
Business continuity	This addresses an organisation's ability to maintain operations and continue to deliver products and services to its customers following a disruptive event.
Cause	Pre-existing conditions that can give rise to a risk.

Change control	A process for managing requests for change in an auditable way, to ensure that only appropriate changes to the project are undertaken, once it has received approval. Also ensures that where changes are authorised, appropriate additional resources are allocated.
Contingency	An amount of time, budget or functionality incorporated into a plan beyond the project team's best estimate of what is needed, to allow for the adverse impact of risks.
Contingency plan	A plan developed to mitigate the outcome of a risk.
Controls	Controls set out how you propose to stick to your plan in the face of the challenges of the real world, and what you will do when reality forces your project to deviate from plan.
Cost Breakdown Structure (CBS)	Hierarchical presentation of project costs, usually derived from the WBS or PBS.
COTS	Commercial Off-The Shelf refers to components or services that can be bought-in complete, without the need for bespoke development. COTS components can reduce project risk.
Crashing the timelines	Making compromises to advance work ahead of schedule, or to catch up following a significant delay.
Critical path	The sequence of tasks in the project that define the shortest time the project can take. Tasks on the critical path, if delayed, will cause a delay in project completion.
Critical Path Analysis (CPA)	The process of finding and evaluating the critical path.
Deliverable	Also called product or output, the things that the project produces (ie, material things or services).
Delphi Technique	Method for estimating and predicting, in which estimators work independently, using any approach they choose. Results and reasoning are collated and presented anonymously to all estimators. Revised estimates are then prepared and the cycle is repeated until either you get a narrow range of estimates, or a major difference in understanding emerges, which you can investigate.
Decision tree	A tool for evaluating the outcomes of a series of decisions.

Appendix B: Glossary   167

Dependency	Some tasks can be completed at any time and are independent of other activities. Others are linked to events like the start or completion of other tasks. These linkages are called dependencies.
Earned Value Analysis (EVA)	A formal methodology for evaluating project performance that takes full account of schedule, budget and delivery performance.
Fixed and variable risks	A fixed risk is one where, if the risk manifests, the disruption is a clearly defined amount of time, cost, functionality, reputational damage, etc. A variable risks give rise to an uncertain level of disruption, dependent upon circumstances.
Gantt Chart	A tool, popularised by Henry Gantt, that helps a project manager to plan, communicate and manage a project. Shows project activities as horizontal bars, with a length that represents the duration of the task, and places them against a fixed timeline.
Gateway, gate or stage-gate	A decision point that brings control and accountability to a project, by forcing an auditable decision before the project proceeds beyond the gateway.
Goal	States the over-arching purpose of the project – what you seek to achieve. Also known as an aim.
Group Think	When a group seeks consensus before it has reached a satisfactory conclusion. Dissenting voices are rejected (or, indeed, often self-censored), so that rational, critical processes fail and the group makes a decision based on what "everyone knows" rather than the strength of the evidence.
Horizon scanning	The process of looking for evidence of factors that will change the risk profile of a project or organisation.
Impact	The change of outcome resulting from a threat or opportunity.
In scope	Everything that is the project's responsibility to do and achieve.
Inherent risk	Risk existing before any action is taken to address it. Compare this to residual risk.

Islands of stability	Periods in the project schedule when only non-critical work is scheduled, to allow contingency time for multiple work streams, thus breaking the critical path.
Issue	Some adverse condition or event that has occurred, or will certainly occur, and so must be managed. Issues can be minor or major concerns.
Likelihood	A measure of the probability of a risk occurring – often based on an interpretation of how often similar risks have occurred in comparable circumstances in the past. Therefore sometimes referred to as frequency.
Maturity	A defined level of organisational capability to deal with risk in an active, auditable and repeatable manner. Maturity models have four or more (most often five) stages, or levels, and a number of criteria for assessing the level you are at.
Milestone	A significant event in the life of the project. Alternatively, a marker of progress (either large or small).
Mitigation	Any action designed to reduce the likelihood or impact of a risk.
Monte Carlo Method	A computational process that uses random statistics to estimate the distribution of possible durations of a project.
M_o_R®	Management of Risk – the UK Government's methodology for risk management. It is maintained by the OGC.
Network chart	A planning tool that shows the logical sequence of project activities.
Objective(s)	These set out the measures of success that you will apply to achieving your goal – typically in terms of time, cost (or budget or resources) and quality standards.
OGC	Office for Government Commerce – the UK Government agency that is responsible for project management in the UK public sector. They are the owners of methodologies that include PRINCE2™ and M_o_R®.
Opportunity	The potential for a benefit to arise from an uncertain event.
Organisational Breakdown Structure (OBS)	Hierarchical presentation of project team members, according to the work they are allocated. Derived from the WBS.
P3M	Stands for Portfolio, Programme and Project Management

Appendix B: Glossary 169

PEST or PESTLE analysis	Stand for Political-Economic-Social-Technological-Legislative-Environmental – commonly used process for screening for broad strategic trends that can create project risks. See also SPECTRES.
Plans	Plans set out how you intend to deliver a project. They address the three main project elements – tasks, time and resources – and describe what needs to be done, how it will be done, when, by whom, with what assets and materials, and how it will be paid for.
Portfolio management	The processes that coordinate the selection, delivery and evaluation of programmes and projects.
PRINCE2™	PRojects IN Controlled Environments. The UK Government's methodology for project management. It is maintained by the OGC.
Product	Also called a deliverable or output, the things that the project produces (material things or events).
Product Breakdown Structure (PBS)	This sets out all of the products (or deliverables) of your project in a structured way – hence articulates the scope of your project.
Programme	A portfolio of projects and initiatives managed together – sharing something critical like joint objectives or a common resource pool.
Programme Evaluation and Review Technique (PERT)	An estimating technique that combines optimistic, best-estimate and pessimistic, worst-estimate predictions to produce an overall estimate of the most likely duration and standard deviation (spread of likely durations) for a project activity.
Programme management	The coordination of interacting, interdependent or related projects.
Project	An endeavour that stands out of the ordinary set of activities. It has a clear start and end point and produces a defined outcome. It is a coordinated set of activities.
Project board	The governing body of a project – ultimately responsible for the oversight and key decision making. Sometimes called the Project Steering Group.
Project brief	Also called Terms of Reference or PID, the project brief defines the parameters of the project.

Project Initiation Document (PID)	Formal document that sets out why the project will be carried out, what it will produce and the plans for how it will do so.
Project lifecycle	Sequence of stages of the project from beginning to end.
Project management	The process of managing a project. This person deploys tools, processes and attitudes that deal with the complexity and uncertainty inherent in a project.
Project manager	Responsible for all aspects of planning and delivering a project.
Project sponsor	This person (or persons) represents the needs of the organisation to the project and the needs of the project to the organisation. Acts as manager to the project manager. Part of the project governance process, the sponsor will either contribute to, or be wholly responsible for, oversight and decision making. Also referred to as Project Executive, Senior Responsible Owner (SRO) or Project Director.
Proximity	How close we are to a potential threat or opportunity. Most often refers to distance in time; can also refer to geographical proximity or emotional proximity.
Quality Assurance (QA)	The process that focuses on ensuring quality is maintained.
Quality Control (QC)	The process that checks to ensure that the quality standards have been met.
Quality Design (QD)	Ensuring quality is prioritised in the design of project deliverables.
Quality Plan	A plan showing how each quality process will operate, what resources will be available and who has responsibility for each aspect of quality.
RACI chart	Responsible, Authority (can authorise sign-off), Consulted, Informed – a chart displaying key project team members and stakeholders.
RAG reporting	Red-Amber-Green designations for project status – also called Traffic Light reporting.
Re-baselining	Creating a new plan from which to work based on current information and abandoning the old plan as a basis for monitoring and controlling your project.

Appendix B: Glossary   171

Residual risk	Risk remaining after action is taken to address it. Compare this to inherent risk.
Risk	Project risk is uncertainty that can affect outcomes. Risk can introduce a positive (opportunity) or negative (threat) change.
Risk appetite	The level of exposure to risk that you are prepared to tolerate.
Risk Breakdown Structure (RBS)	A hierarchical representation of all risks, starting with a few broad areas and breaking each down into ever more specific risks.
Risk capacity	The level of exposure to risk that your project is able to tolerate.
Risk exposure	The value that you are placing at risk.
Risk map	Also called a risk matrix, this is a chart showing risks plotted on two axes, most commonly likelihood and impact.
Risk owner	The person responsible for the planning and execution of actions to manage a specific risk.
Risk Potential Review (RPR)	A structured analysis of different aspects of your project that will give you a measure of how risky it is overall.
Risk register	Formal document and management tool that records all risks identified by the project team, along with the team's assessment of the risks, plans to manage the risks and progress against the plans.
Risky shift	As a result of Group Think, the group endorses a risk position significantly greater or lesser than the average level of risk that each member of the group would have taken individually.
RMS (Root Mean Square) method	A statistical technique to calculate a range of quantitative estimates of aggregate risk from a number of independent risks.
Scenario planning	Identifying a range of possible future outcomes based on uncertain events, as a basis for testing out and refining plans.
Scope	All that the project must do and create. It can be expressed in terms of activities, articulated by the WBS, or in terms of deliverables, articulated by the PBS.

Scope creep	The tendency for people to sneak extra work and outputs into a project's list of responsibilities. This can cause a project to fail under the burden of additional work.
Severity	Numerical measure of impact.
SPECTRES	Stands for Social-Political-Economic-Competitive-Technological-Regulatory-Environmental-Security. Enhanced version of PESTLE analysis used to identify sources of risk.
SRO	Senior Responsible Owner – a PRINCE2 term for the Project Sponsor.
Stakeholder	Anyone with an interest in your project – whether affected by its outcome or process, or with an ability to affect its outcome or process.
Steering group	Any group of users, suppliers or experts who feed considered opinions into the project.
SWOT analysis	Strengths-Weaknesses-Opportunities-Threats. A method for evaluating strategic risk and level of readiness.
TCQ Triangle	The Time-Cost-Quality Triangle. Also known as the Iron Triangle, Triangle of Balance or the Triple Constraint.
Threat	The potential for an adverse outcome to arise from an uncertain event.
Transfer	Creating a mechanism by which another party will accept the consequences of a risk.
Version control	A process for controlling the version of a project document to ensure team members can readily ensure that the version they are working from is the most up-to-date. Project documents should have a name and version number on each page.
Work Breakdown Structure (WBS)	Formal tool that breaks down the project (the work) into a structure, allowing a firm inventory of tasks, in a logical hierarchy.
Work stream	A subset of the WBS that is allocated to a single manager, the work stream leader.

APPENDIX C: LEARN MORE

BELOW IS A BY NO MEANS EXHAUSTIVE list of books that I have found useful. The books are arranged in order of significance to me, beginning with risk management titles and followed by associated topics.

Tom Kendrick. *Identifying and Managing Project Risk: Essential Tools for Failure-Proofing Your Project* **(Amacom).** This is my favourite book on project risk management. It has a comprehensive scope at a slightly more technical level than *Risk Happens!* and uses the Panama Canal as a rolling case study.

Chris Chapman and Stephen Ward. *Project Risk Management: Processes, Techniques and Insights* **(John Wiley & Sons).** This also offers a comprehensive coverage of risk management, but is more academic in tone.

Edmund H. Conrow. *Effective Risk Management: Some keys to success* **(American Institute of Aeronautics & Astronautics).** Another excellent and wide ranging book on project risk management, which goes into some areas in more detail than *Risk Happens!* Conrow's description of the risk management process is the most similar to my own of any books I have read.

Office for Government Commerce. *Management of Risk: Guidance for Practitioners* **(Stationery Office).** This is a well-researched resource on risk management in all contexts (not specifically in projects), with an emphasis on good governance. It is an essential reference for anyone working at a high level in the UK public sector.

Project Management Institute. *Practice Standard for Project Risk Management* **(Project Management Institute).** The PMI is the US membership body for project managers and their body of knowledge (the PMBOK). This book contains the core curriculum for their Project Management Professional standard. This Practice Standard extends the PMBOK's coverage of risk management.

Risk Toolkit – How to take care of risk in volunteering: a guide for organisations **(The Institute for Volunteering Research and Volunteering England).** If you work in the voluntary sector, this very helpful 60-page pamphlet is essential. You can download a pdf from the Volunteering England website.

Peter L. Bernstein. *Against the Gods: The Remarkable Story of Risk* **(John Wiley & Sons).** Not about project risk at all, but a great read if you want to understand the history of our understanding of risk, from an expert in the financial investment industry.

Gerd Gigerenzer. *Reckoning with Risk* **(Penguin).** This is a popular paperback that will help you understand the statistical nature of risk. It is filled with compelling examples of the sort of risks we hear about every day in the news.

Dan Gardner. *Risk: The Science and Politics of Fear* **(Virgin).** Another popular paperback, this one focuses on the psychology of our perceptions of risk, and its impact within the context of the political process.

James Surowiecki. *The Wisdom of Crowds: Why the Many are Smarter than the Few* **(Abacus).** Essential reading for team problem solvers and decision makers; this book shows you how to make wise decisions in a group, rather than dangerous ones.

Mary Douglas and Aaron Wildavsky. *Risk and Culture: An Essay on the Selection of Technical and Environmental Dangers* **(University of California Press).** Sets out the Cultural Theory of Risk that I outline in Chapter 12.

Gary Klein. *The Power of Intuition* **(Crown Business).** Gary Klein is one of the foremost experts on business decision making and this book is filled with fascinating tips and ideas, including his "pre-mortem" exercise for assessing the risks inherent in any decision.

Mike Clayton. *The Handling Resistance Pocketbook* **(Management Pocketbooks).** Filled with essential tips and techniques for dealing with stakeholder resistance and resistance to change.

Mike Clayton. *The Management Models Pocketbook* **(Management Pocketbooks).** Three models outlined here are of particular relevance to risk managers: Tuckman's model of group development, Adair's model of team leadership and Boyd's OODA Loop.

Mike Clayton. *Brilliant Project Leader* **(Prentice Hall).** Focuses on the people aspects of project management, employing the same underlying processes as *Risk Happens!*

ABOUT THE AUTHOR

Risk management is in Mike Clayton's genes, inherited from his father. When he first learned about formal risk management methods, Mike found the processes and tools intuitive and familiar. On all of the projects Mike has managed, he has emphasised the importance of good risk management to anyone who would listen – or who had no choice!

Mike is now a business speaker and author. He focuses on project management, getting things done, integrating complex change and effective influence and decision making. Mike got much of his experience from 12 years at Deloitte Consulting, where he specialised in the delivery and integration of complex change in a diverse range of private and public sector organisations.

His experience includes a leading role in a £60 million programme for BAA plc, two major projects with The Post Office, an extensive infrastructure project for Transport for London, and keystone projects for Ministry of Defence, General Motors and local government in the UK. All of these involved significant and very different risks; all were delivered to schedule, budget and specification.

Working in and leading a wide variety of highly successful teams has given Mike valuable insights into organisational change, team-working and leadership skills. He presents a personal point of view and real tools from 20 years of consulting and management experience. This is combined with knowledge gained from working and training with some outstanding leaders in business and personal development.

Shift Happens! is Mike's blog about projects, risk and change. You can read it on the Risk Happens! website, at *www.riskhappens.co.uk*.